*Welcome the Birds
to Your Home*

Welcome
THE BIRDS

TO YOUR HOME

by Jane & Will Curtis

with illustrations by John Sill

:: A Greenemont Book ::

The Stephen Greene Press, Brattleboro, Vt.

for Dorothy

This book has been produced in the United States of America. It is designed by Robert R. Anderson, and published by the Stephen Greene Press, Brattleboro, Vermont 05301

LIBRARY OF CONGRESS CATALOGING IN PUBLICATION DATA

Curtis, Jane, 1918–
  Welcome the birds to your home.

  "A Greenemont book."
  Bibliography: p.
  Includes index.
  1. Birds—North America. 2. Bird watching—
North America. 3. Birds, Attracting of.
I. Curtis, Will, 1917–   *joint author.*
II. Title.
QL681.C9   598.2'073   79-20819
ISBN 0-8289-0353-0
ISBN 0-8289-0354-9 pbk.

Contents

Acknowledgments

As we were the rankest of neophytes when we began to welcome birds, so were we when we sat down to write this book. It would never have seen the light of day without the help and encouragement of many people. We especially wish to thank:

Mrs. Irene Godfrey of Natchez, Mississippi, for her gracious hospitality and for generously sharing her vast store of ornithological knowledge. Dr. Philip Schultz of Santa Fe, New Mexico, for the opportunity to visit him and his eagle/hawk hospital. Tom Martin, New York City, bird photographer par excellence, who taught us all we know of that art. David Laughlin of Woodstock, Vermont, who has been endlessly patient on bird walks. And particularly Sarah Laughlin of Woodstock, Vermont, Director of the Vermont Institute of Natural Science, who took time from her busy schedule to read this manuscript. John Sill of Franklin, North Carolina, for his excellent art work. Finally, we are grateful to Janet Greene, editor and friend, who pulled it all together.

Throughout the text we have followed the usage of the American Ornithologists' Union for the proper names of birds, and *Hortus Third* (New York, 1976) for the common names of plants.

Jane and Will Curtis
Sugarbrook Farm
Hartland, Vermont

Red-winged blackbird

That Blackbird

It was one of those mornings. One of those bad mornings. Everybody knows about them. Coffee not quite hot enough, cat whining underfoot, daughter whining about Miss Jenkins, the mean math teacher. And hovering over all, the bad witch of suburbia, Lateness. Late for school, the car pool, the train. Late. Got to run! Throw cat outdoors, shove daughter after her, toast in mouth, one arm in coat. Husband cramming papers into briefcase, wife galloping in the rear.

This is the picture of our small family, head down,

charging into another day. It was a March morning, squelchy and dank. No one was in a mood to be enthusiastic about anything except getting to our destinations on time. But we had a surprise in store. And it changed us. It started in a very small way. There we were, three of us, oblivious to anything but our own concerns, harried and rather cross with each other, Jane, Will, and Katie, and wondering why our lives had to be one constant gallop.

Then, from the mist overhead came a trilled *ok-a-lee, ok-a-lee*. A bird, jet black except for a startling scarlet shoulder patch, flew by. We were late, we were hurrying, but for a second we all stood and listened to the bird call *ok-a-lee* from the top of a tree near by. Then we were off again. That was the very small start, lasting only a second, on a journey that still continues.

Our home Typical city dwellers we were when we moved into an old house away from the urban scene. The suburbs had swept around it. Its fields and woods had been divided into "estates." But to us urbanites it was country. The rambling eighteenth-century house still sat surrounded by shaggy lawns and decrepit apple trees. In the old barn were horse stalls, some musty hay in mows overhead, and a cavernous grain bin filled with spider webs.

Of course our friends predicted that we'd be back after the first winter. Those delights of late theater nights, those long lazy Sunday breakfasts, the delis, museums, good schools: how could we be without them? Surely the PTA and the men's sporting clubs would be poor substitutes. Snow shoveling would bring on heart attacks, and putting up jellies would soon be tiresome and anyhow they probably wouldn't jell.

But we moved in in the fall, enchanted with the soft

autumnal days and our romantic house. We spent the winter coping with drafty floors, recalcitrant furnaces, and leaky storm windows.

In the muddy spring when we had time to think, doubts assailed us. Were our friends right after all? Were we really suited to this life of galloping commuting, chilly fingers, smoking chimneys? This was the family mood when that bird with the shoulder patch flew by.

At dinner that night, back together from office, shop, and school, our daughter Katie, aged nine, said, "Mom, Dad, guess what?" We couldn't. "Remember that bird? The one with the red?" Yes, we remembered, a tiny incident that for a second made us stop and listen. "Well, Miss Riley, our science teacher, pinned up pictures of birds that will be coming here this spring and played a record for us to hear their songs. And that bird was one of them, and I heard that song again. *Ok-a-lee.* He's a red-winged blackbird. Let's see if we can hear him tomorrow."

There we were. We had started on our journey together. It was a pretty small start, one red-winged blackbird, but it was a beginning.

Well, the next morning there that bird was again, trilling away from the top of an apple tree. The song seemed to fit in well with the day, for somehow it evoked spring. Spring! Could we perhaps smell a hint of wet but warming earth? Did the brown patch of grass take on just a tinge of green? The March mood lifted to give a glimpse of April's coming. Bulbs would be up, seeds could be put in the earth. Perhaps after all we could cope with the drafts and snowdrifts.

It was Katie's Miss Riley who got us to do something about what was happening all about us. Every time we hurried up across the lawn in the morning we took time to look for our friend, and at the same time noticed other sorts of birds, flitting about, bigger, smaller, some brownish, others reddish, all uttering sounds, squeaks, and songs. "Ask Miss Riley, Katie, what that bird with the white streaks on the wings is." At night Katie would dutifully read from her notes that Miss Riley said that if the bird had white wing-bars it might be a flycatcher, but that our description really didn't seem to fit any bird that she knew of.

At last Miss Riley sent home with Katie a gentle hint: Perhaps we might consider buying a bird guide? Katie seemed to be interested, and we were asking questions that could be better answered by looking them up for ourselves. The local bookstore had a section devoted to nature where we would be sure to find something to help.

It did appear to be a sensible idea. The air seemed to be filled with more and more sorts of birds all the time. Why do identification at long range?

The next day being Saturday, it was, as in all suburbia, sacred to the weekly run to the town dump. On *Bird guides* the way home we ventured into the village bookshop for the first time. The city stores we had patronized may have had larger inventories but could hardly match this one for informed and willing help. Will soon found the nature section, where the proprietor had laid in a goodly supply. The trouble was, all the books looked so intriguing. In fascination I turned the pages of a huge volume on the eagles of the world while Will whistled at the jeweled hummingbirds pictured in the beautiful book he was holding. "Look, Mom, Dad, see, there's a book on crows and one on robins. Miss Riley has told us about all those. Can't we get these books, can't we?" Katie tried to hold them all.

The owner strolled over. Wasn't this a rather large selection of books just on birds for a village bookstore, we asked him. Not at all, he told us; bird guides sell year in and out, and more of them all the time. In fact, it was hard to keep them in stock. He gently and firmly removed from our hands the huge eagle book and the one on hummingbirds and those on the private lives of jays, crows, and robins. He recommended field guides to bird identification. We finally bought two in paperback and followed his advice about Katie being old enough to use them. We could hardly wait to get home to identify for ourselves the birds who were so busily taking up residence on our land. We were hooked.

Another quantum leap took place shortly thereafter. We had noticed in our new awareness something important. We couldn't sleep in the morning. A perfectly dreadful cacophony of squeaks, squawks, and piercing whistles was occurring just outside our bedroom window. We had read of the divine bird dawn-chorus that English writers are always going on about. Surely this uproar couldn't be termed a chorus? But it was certainly dawn. Early morning ashcan-banging and sirens one somehow can get used to, but this shrieking was unbearable. The bird guides were no help. Leaky old houses we were learning to cope with, but lack of sleep couldn't go on.

Unwelcome serenade

The problem was solved in this way. We are blessed with a local store that within its capacious walls manages to stock hardware, gardening material, and paints in addition to its grocery section. As a result you can see everybody there: the plumber in for a fitting, a dog-fancier buying a new dog mattress, or housewives pushing carts around. Just everyone turns up there once a day, and there is sure to be someone who can answer questions on whom to consult about mice in the eaves or how to make a casserole. It is our information booth.

And one day, sure enough, standing in line was the local wise man, a present-day John Burroughs. "What can we do about that frightful chorus of insane birds?" "You own the old Varney place, don't you, with all the old apple trees?" We allowed as how we did. "Well, you have starlings living neck by jowl with you." We certainly agreed with that. "Haven't you noticed that your old trees have lots and lots of holes in them?" No, we really hadn't noticed holes in the old trees. We were probably too busy noticing the holes in the old house. "You know, don't you, that different sorts of birds build different kinds of nests?" We looked at each other and shook our heads. We didn't know that. There was so much we didn't know. We really hadn't thought about it. We assumed that all those birds flying about had raised their young in the kind of bedraggled snow-covered nest tucked in a bush outside the back door. The expert regarded us kindly. He was used to neophytes who had moved from the city.

Starlings   "Well, starlings are hole-nesters." He shook his head. "When I think of that idiot back in 1890 who brought eighty of the noisy creatures from Europe and set them free in New York's Central Park I'd like to tell him a thing or two! Those starlings have increased by the millions and spread from Hudson Bay to Mexico and California, competing for all the best holes with our native birds who are hole-nesters too.

"But don't get me going on man's interference with the environment," he went on. "I'll tell you about that later if you're really interested. Right now you want to know what to do so you can get some sleep in the early morning. If you can't put up with the racket, cut down the trees. Or fill up the holes. But do take some time to look at the starlings; they're not just dingy black. They're really beautifully iridescent green and purple around the shoulders now that they're in spring plumage. And remember that birds differ just as humans do in their notions of what makes a good place in which to bring up young."

Well, that was an idea to chew over. Do city folk ever have time or reason to think of any other beings except the other humans of whom they're so constantly aware?

The trees didn't come down, of course. Their ancient spirits were too pervasive. Instead, the three of us scurried about with buckets of tree cement, filling up any hole that might entice a starling couple to move in bag and baggage and start raising a family. Evidently we were just in time, for they hadn't actually begun to build. We weren't breaking up any happy homes. The starlings perched on the gnarled branches and watched with interest. But we did feel a bit guilty, and in the end left a hole-ridden tree at the edge of our property for their apartment house.

Just as well, it turned out. Starlings are notoriously bad housekeepers, leaving their excrement to pile up in a most unsanitary fashion. As for their noise, we have learned almost to appreciate its ingenuity. What other bird can combine the twang of a jew's-harp, squeak of a rusty gate-hinge, cluck of a hen, and rattle of a wire spring, all interspersed with a short, sweet whistle?

We learned a lot that spring. One of the attractions for us was the big old barn, wonderful to store things in, wonderful to play in. We were filled with pride at actually owning a barn. It was ours. Then we discovered that hundreds of barn swallows considered it theirs. They'd flown thousands of miles looking forward to summer in that wonderful barn! For generations before we came, their ancestors had built and rebuilt mud-and-clay nests on the large crossbeams

barn
swallows

A red-wing's home

above the dusty haymow. The farmer's wagons had suffered no damage from mud and bird droppings. But when we moved in with our new suburban pride and joy, a station wagon, our relation with the swallows changed quickly. Its glossy surface was mottled with splotches of clay interspersed with random bits of straw and bird manure. Not an object to be proud of as it stood in the station parking lot.

One Sunday morning Will appeared in the house nervously holding a .22 rifle.

"Where did you get that?"

"It's Frank Clay's, and I'm going to shoot those damned birds!"

Great consternation. I felt for the swallows, but I shared Will's despair for our indispensable car. Katie at once set up a high wailing. Will determinedly strode up to the barn, the women following. The big door was slid-to behind him. Katie wrung her hands. I, by this time on the birds' side, shouted, "Don't be melodramatic!" A silence ensued except for the nervous twittering of the swallows. Katie, with her hands over her ears, suddenly stopped crying. To our utter astonishment a pane in the window above the big door quietly tipped out and drifted slantways to the ground, where it lay intact. Behind it streamed the swallows. The barn door opened. Will walked out and across the road to Frank Clay's to return the .22.

Now we simply leave the station wagon outside while the swallows are raising their children.

Another lesson began on a warm day at the end of May when Katie wandered off to the very edge of our property where a wet, low spot filled with bulrushes joined our land to our neighbor's. They were newcomers also, and also viewed the little marshy place with suspicion as a breeding ground for all sorts of undesirable wildlife. Snakes, newts—who knew what would crawl out of it? Together we made plans to have it filled in.

That night Katie said she'd seen our bird sitting there on a bulrush top and singing. She wasn't really sure it was the very same bird, for there appeared to be others, but they were red-wings.

The next day she and a friend tried to creep through the rushes, but the male instantly changed his singing to such an alarmed clicking that they backed away. Just as well, for Agnes, the cat, had followed the search party.

After that the birds were left alone to raise their families in peace. We decided that they deserved privacy just as much as we did.

The males stopped singing and flying about with their bright patches flashing when the summer's broods had grown, and we forgot about the blackbirds. In the fall, however, when school started, Katie told Miss Riley about our wet place (which we had not gotten around to filling in). She asked if she might bring her science class to see if the nests could be found.

So one bright September day the children streamed down past the trees to the swamp, frisking like colts, Miss Riley not looking much older. And Agnes came galloping behind, catching leaves.

In the swamp the children stepped carefully—for they had been well schooled—holding notebooks in hand, looking quietly. One small booted foot was just coming down when another child gave a warning yell. There it was, looking like a clump of reeds near the base of the rushes. When we gathered about and looked we could see that the base of the rushes had been interwoven with stout grasses and weeds to make a cuplike foundation that was lined with finer stems. Later, after all had had a chance to see it, and notes

had been carefully jotted down, we sat under the apple trees and Miss Riley led us in a discussion of the private life of the red-winged blackbird.

I never imagined that there was so much to know, and how many things we hadn't noticed about this bird. To begin with, that dank March morning when we saw him for the first time, he was alone. We hadn't seen the female because she wasn't there. Males arrive first, in flocks, almost three weeks before the females turn up, to look over the situation and establish territory. They may have their ideas of a proper nest site, but the female is firm about the spot she prefers and does most of the nest-building, as is true with most birds.

We marveled that so low a nest could escape birds' enemies, all those creatures that depend on flesh for survival. How could Mrs. Blackbird sit for twelve days incubating her eggs, and as many more raising the nestlings, and still not attract the attention of Agnes and all her feline friends and relations? One of the answers lies in the female's drab and streaked *Camouflage* feathers. They are her protection as she incubates the eggs in the well-concealed spot, since she blends in perfectly with the sun-dappled rushes. And the young in the nest look like her: another bit of camouflage, for the adolescent males have to wait a year until they can wear the bright scarlet epaulets of their father.

When Miss Riley told us that all the red-wings in the country would in four months eat 16,200,000,000 larvae of destructive bugs and worms, we decided then and there that the wet spot would not be filled in! We would be more than happy to have our small flock of birds eat any of the pests they wanted.

Red-winged blackbirds who built nests in swamps, starlings who liked holes in trees, and swallows who flew in the spring right to our barn—why did they like such different places? What else were they up to? What other birds were around? These hitherto unasked questions and our adventures together in finding answers gave us a common interest, a reason for being alert while working outdoors. Our ears and eyes became sharpened. The sense that other living beings also lived on what we had thought of as our land made *Stewardship* us aware that we were only stewards of our property. That in a sense we didn't "own" land, it belonged to all who inhabited it.

Thus the first year went by quickly, so engrossed were we with learning to live in the old farmhouse and so fascinated by the creatures living there with us.

One late winter evening Rob Jarvis, the wise man who had become a good friend, was having dinner with us. "Almost time for your red-wing, isn't it, Katie?"

Black-capped chickadee

Bird Identification
Can Be Easy

Why did Katie's red-wing come back to our swamp, the starlings to the ancient apple trees, and the swallows to the barn that their ancestors knew? We hadn't done anything to provide these attractions—the marshy, reedy ground, the holes, and the rafters; they were just there waiting for the birds.

"Attractive; to attract . . ." We knew that for years people had been throwing out crusts on snow, but surely there was more to attracting birds than that. Why couldn't we do something that would make them want to live here, build their nests here? What did the word "nest" mean to us? Shelter, of course. Just what the word "home" means. It suggests a place where we can have rest, protection, food and drink, and bring *Welcoming birds* up young. Why couldn't we make our home one that would welcome birds in the same way? A place of attractive shelter?

Full of springtime zeal we hurried to tell this to Rob Jarvis. "Well, that's certainly a novel way of going about the bird business—attracting them by offering them shelter! Most folks start via the crust route and then graduate to feeders stuffed with food like a supermarket, a more sophisticated one every winter, it seems. You see the darndest contraptions hanging around in people's yards. It beats me how a bird ever figures out how to use them.

"Well, now you're proposing to do it differently. No reason why not; shelter is certainly one of the most important factors in keeping birds going, just as important as food and water."

We beamed at his approval, but then he added this: "Just remember that making a place attractive entails a lot of knowledge. It's learning why certain birds live in a hole and others nest on the ground. Why grubs and caterpillars are like T-bone steaks to one, while another species will relish thistle seed. There's pruning, planting, and pools to learn about. And to find all this out, first you're going to have to learn to identify the birds that live around here or nest here. Then the rest will follow. Start by getting binoculars. And good luck!"

Rob warned us that we really didn't realize on what an adventure we were embarking. When we looked back I believe we were following the Chinese adage that says a journey of even a thousand miles begins with a single step. If we'd known what lay ahead down that road, and what a project it was going to be, perhaps we would never have taken that step. But no adventure worth its salt is any fun if it's all planned beforehand. Prepackaged tours are apt to be boring and soon over. This adventure, this journey, will last as long as we live.

Lest anyone is afraid to start, let me say that the

next step follows as naturally as walking after the first step is taken. By the time you're well into it, you don't want to turn back anyway; you're having too much fun. Learning to identify birds leads to knowledge of where to find them, where and how they nest, how they raise their young. By then you're well on the way to looking critically at your own place to see what can be done to welcome the birds.

A birder's day

But for us, at least, that first step of learning to see and know birds was a long one, entailing many frustrating hours. Also some unforgettable sunrises and two weary bodies. For there are many hours in a bird watcher's day. It begins an hour before sunrise because birds start then to move about on their business. By midmorning, when suburban weekend slugabeds get up, the birds are sitting resting comfortably on a branch somewhere, conserving energy for the big job of finding food for their families. By eleven o'clock the bird watcher is finished watching birds and he or she is free to paint shutters or lay flagstone walks. That's where our weary bodies came from. The frustration and sunrises were side effects of birding. There were compensations. When we'd stumble into the dew-laden spring morning and before we'd had time to regret our warm beds we would feel ourselves part of the mysterious life all around us. The young leaves were unfolding like a baby's hand, spiders' webs were strung with mist like pearls. In the pale light the birds were playing their parts as members of an invisible orchestra. And that was what was amiss: They were all around us, but they were invisible to us.

A little stripy thing would bob its head at us, peck tentatively at the bark and bounce around the other side of the tree. Will or I would let out a long exasperated sigh.

"There it goes again! It's just like all these birds.

They won't hold still one second. Every time I get to a spot where it is and get the glasses up and then get them focused, off it goes. It's enough to make me wonder if we're capable of this bird business. And another thing, why do there have to be so many different kinds of birds?"

Back in the city before we became country folks we used to laugh at the birders. All those dedicated ladies, some of whom actually looked like birds. And the hearty types who would stand for days in bogs, huge binoculars apparently part of their faces. And here we were standing in a bog with glasses fixed to our eyes. And we weren't doing very well. The sheer numbers daunted us, not to speak of the unhelpful way birds changed their plumage. Why couldn't males and females look alike? Cats and dogs do.

The most disheartening aspect of the bird world was that everyone else seemed to have all the salient facts stored in his or her head like a computer's memory bank. It was most discouraging.

The low point in our voyage of discovery was the day we rashly joined a bird walk organized by a local *A bird walk* nature club. It was spring migration and, worse luck for us, the warblers were passing through. Warblers are small, flitting birds, hard to spot, who migrate from Middle America, mostly east of the Rockies, into the northern United States and into Canada. We learned later that it would have been much worse in the fall, for then they have a terrible tendency to look alike.

As neophytes we were paired off with a couple formidably garlanded with glasses. They strolled ahead with an air of nonchalant competence, Will and I humbly in the rear.

An infinitesimal flash and their glasses would be whipped up instantly. Excited whispers of, "It's a blue-winged." "Yup, I've got him." Will and I strained to see something besides fuzzy leaves and branches. When our mentors showed us its picture in the guide we couldn't see that it differed much at all from the bird portrayed next to it.

This went on all afternoon. We stumbled along in their wake trying to find the last bird they had spotted only to have them find another almost at once. We would memorize color details only to forget them the instant the bird was seen again. It was an humiliating two hours. It seemed to stretch on forever.

Finally Will whispered to fake it. "Just tell them you've got it, for heaven's sake. But be sure to point the glasses in the right direction. We can't go on like this all afternoon having them stop and be patient with us just because we seem to be idiots."

There's a happy ending to our story, though. We did learn; and easily, too. A few months after our disastrous bird walk we spent a fall weekend camping in a national park. The bulletin announced a bird-watching workshop. "There's nothing to lose," said Will. At the appointed time we found ourselves with some others who admitted warily that they were just as shaky about the bird world as we were.

"Cheer up," said the young naturalist-cum-park-ranger as he passed out information sheets and guidebooks. "I promise that by the time you leave this group you'll really know how to identify birds and you'll never forget."

He started by assuring us that it was very unlikely that the particular bird we were looking at would be 100 percent like the picture in the book. Birds of the

Birds and pictures   same species vary somewhat in plumage according to the season, their age, and where they're found. The artist who painted the picture had to incorporate the variations of age and geographical area into one generalized picture. As a matter of interest, that's why paintings are used in field guides instead of photographs. The descriptions may call for a buffy breast, but in the part of the country in which we might see him the bird might be a lot more greyish. If we knew how to look for points that never change, no matter how old the bird was or in what state of plumage, we'd be able to make a pretty educated stab at finding out what it was.

"The identification points never change," he continued. "They will get you into the right section of the book, too, without fumbling through the pages."

The Identification Points

"First of all, the size. Compare it to a bird you know. Is it bigger or smaller than a robin? Now you already have a fix on it, for you know its size approximately.

"Next, the tail shape. Is it notched, square-ended, *Size, Tail, Bill* pointed, or round-tipped?

"Then what about the bill? Does the bird have a long probing beak, a stout seed-cracker, or does it have a sharp insect-eating tweezer? Perhaps a hooked tearing beak?

"Do you see that you've gotten three very important things that never change? Now here's one more: behavior. Does it hop on the ground, fly in swoops, investigate a tree by going up, or down? Behavior is very important.

"Of course," he added, "you've got to be sure that the bird you have identified really belongs to the area. Birds always seek the same sort of habitat, and knowing what kind it prefers is another clue to identification."

Then he gave us a three-minute test. He brought from a box a stuffed bird, held it up for a minute, reminding us to remember to look for size, tail and

beak shapes first, then any color markings. He gave us a description of how the bird behaved and told us to start the identification.

It was remarkable that at the end of three minutes all of us had gotten the bird into the correct family and genus if not the exact species. And all of us nailed the next three birds right on the button.

"There, you see? You can do it. But here's more advice before I turn you loose on the bird world. Take time really to memorize the parts of the bird so that you can correctly describe a bird to another person. Who knows, you may see something unusual one day, and you'll make a much stronger case for your identification if you know how to use the correct terminology when describing the bird."

His last piece of advice startled us for a moment. He told us to keep our bird guide in our pocket!

"Go about your identification this way," he said. "Spot the bird. Say aloud to yourself or to another person the first three points of identification: size, tail, and beak shape. Then the behavior and color markings. If you say them aloud, you're more apt to remember them. Then write them down on some paper—and only then take out the guide and start to hunt for the bird's description.

"What you've probably been doing is whipping out that book when you first see the bird, and you'll have forgotten the characteristics before you find anything in the book. Usually by the time you've dropped the glasses you can't remember whether the tail is notched or how the beak looked. And then you're confronted with all these choices in the book. If you do it my way, you've narrowed it down before you have opened the book. Now you're on your own."

Next morning Will and I identified three birds all by ourselves! It was so easy. Why had no one told us of this before?

Learning the Birds' Calls

There's another trick to identifying birds in the summer when they're likely to be hidden in dense foliage, particularly those who live in the woods, and that is to memorize certain catchy phrases or syllables that make up their songs and calls. Bird songs are just as distinctive as behavior, markings, and color.

New Englanders call the white-throated sparrow, common from Manitoba to Newfoundland, from Minnesota to Connecticut, the "Peabody bird" because they say he is calling for *Sam Peabody, Peabody, Peabody*. Peabody's cousin, the desert-loving black-throated sparrow, says sweetly *cheat, cheat cheeee*, which goes either down or up as the bird sees fit.

In the deciduous woods of most of the United States the upside-down bird, the white-breasted nuthatch, simply says in a nasal voice *yank* or *hank*, while the white-winged dove among the cacti of the Southwest asks plaintively *who cooks for who?*

Drink your tea says the rufous-sided towhee to Americans and Canadians alike. The purple finch, also at home in the open woodlands of North America, calls *come to me, I am here*.

From Manitoba to Quebec, from Missouri to New Jersey, the rose-breasted grosbeak calls exuberantly *whooperee, boys, let's go!* In the western provinces and states the black-headed grosbeak, his near relative, agrees and repeats the call. As do their mates: a most unusual occurrence, for very seldom do the females sing the male songs.

The veery, deep in the dim woods of Canada and the northern United States is almost impossible to see, because he is a ventriloquist; but his song of two rolling notes with a descending spiral at the end is easy to remember, once heard.

A common bird, the red-eyed vireo, ranges over

most of North America's deciduous woods, talks all day long, asking questions and immediately answering them. Some believe he's saying *see me, look up, 'way up*.

Because the warblers are busy little birds, hopping rapidly through the branches, they're difficult to see, so learning some of their songs is a great help.

Bird voices

The most common song of the chestnut-sided warbler of southern Canada and the United States is *sweet, sweet, sweet, I'll switch you*, with emphasis on the last two words.

Teacher, teacher teach! the ovenbird orders, in the woods east of the Rockies; but his cousin, the northern water thrush who nests in Canada and the northern United States, starts out in ringing notes, ending in *chew-chew-chew-chew*, descending in pitch. The Louisiana water thrush sings three clear slurred notes and then has a series of dropping twitters. All three birds are really warblers.

The magnolia warbler, who flies to Canada's evergreen forests to nest, says *wheato, wheato wheatee* with the final "ee" rising; but it may also say *wheato, wheato wheatsip* with the "sip" descending.

All across America the yellowthroat says *whichity, whichity, whichity,* and the black-throated blue warbler of the East says simply *I am la-zy*.

Make up your own words when you hear a bird you know. Or better yet, invest in a song record and try to fit words to the songs; or make notes that approximate the sounds, with arrows indicating upward and downward trills. You'll be surprised how many birds you'll be able to identify even if you can't see them.

At the end of the summer we weren't much further along towards our goal of improving the place by providing shelter, but at least we had a fairly good idea of the species of birds that nested in our area.

Rose-breasted grosbeak

Nests on the Ground,
Nests in the Treetops

"They build a ratty nest." We human beings peered up through the leafless branches of the dogwood at a ramshackle assemblage of twigs. The rose-breasted grosbeak about whose nest Miss Riley was making such disparaging remarks had long since departed for the warmer climate of Central America.

"It's a platform nest, a very loosely built twiggy floor laid across a fork in a branch, with a nest built on top. And look how flimsy the nest is, so carelessly woven together. When there are eggs in it you can see them right up through the spaces when you stand below. They're pale blue, spotted with browns, about four of them. What's unusual is that the male helps to incubate. He develops a brood patch; and, even more unusual, he sometimes sings while sitting there."

"What's so unusual about that?"

"Katie, look up the picture of a rose-breasted in your guide. There, see that vivid bird? He's all sharp contrasts, black and white, and he's got that big triangular rose patch on his breast. Do you see what I'm getting at?"

"You mean he's hard to miss?"

Male coloring   "That's it exactly. Most male birds stay away from the eggs as much as they can. They don't dare to attract attention to the nest. But see how beautifully camouflaged the female is, blending in with the lights and shadows, all streaky browns and whites. This bright-colored character, the male, actually sits and sings on the eggs! He's like certain artistic types who don't care what kind of mess the place is in as long as they can paint or sculpt—or, in the case of this grosbeak, sing."

I had a suspicion that Will didn't sympathize with the rose-breasted grosbeak's life style. Will, an actuary, cared how his place looked,

The scarlet tanager, another platform-nester, was a sloppy carpenter too, but he was a bit more comfort-loving. His nests were lined with a little grass or lichen to fill in the chinks. One would think the infant grosbeaks and tanagers might be uncomfortable in such cradles, but somehow, Miss Riley said, the parents managed to bring them up in the rickety affairs.

She strolled on, continuing her informal lecture. We knew about the blackbird's nest nearly on the ground, but did we know that the oriole swings his hammock at least thirty feet in the air? It's too bad that orioles nest so high up, because it would be wonderful to see the female knit her bag together. Miss Riley had seen them fly by holding in their beaks a long piece of straw, which they use to make a grassy collar suspended from a branch tip. Then they work together to hang from it an open network pouch about eight inches long. Finishing it off is the female's specialty. She pushes in a long strand of grass, hops inside to pull the strand in, and then pushes it out again. She's really weaving it.

Unfortunately, we didn't have on our place their favorite tree, an elm. Its drooping branches are treasured by orioles because they know instinctively that squirrels and cats don't care to trust their weight to the elm's slender tips. Of course if they can't find an elm the orioles will use willows or maples or the tops of apple trees. Later, not far away, on our way to work on a winter's morning, we spotted a little grey bag topped with snow: an oriole's nest, hanging far above the road.

Miss Riley explained that most perching birds, the ones that frequent our gardens, don't weave their nests but work the material together by using their feet and bodies. The robins, whose nest-building can be seen rather easily, start by collecting straw, leaves, little roots, and strong grass, and putting them where they will be well supported, since the finished nest will be heavy. When enough of this material has been worked together, the female will go to the nearest muddy place and bring back soft mud in her beak. This is plastered into the dry grasses until they are well soaked. Then she gets into the nest and shapes it by turning round and round until it fits her body. Before the mud is hardened the nest is lined with soft grasses.

Nest construction

We had to be content with the oriole's nest down the road, but we found on our place a different one almost as dramatic. Sharp-eyed Katie spotted it in a shadbush in the fall. It was about ten feet from the ground and she would never have found it if she hadn't been looking for nests. After a stepladder and clippers were brought into play, we had it in our hands, together with the branch it was fastened to. The miniature affair had been made of small twiglets thickly woven with grasses on the inside, and, most wonderful, the cup had been suspended from a small V-shaped branch by cobwebs. If you're one who doubts that cobwebs can be used the way a contractor uses steel cables in building, try to get a filament of the stuff off your hands. Not only sticky, it's also surprisingly strong. We took the nest to Rob Jarvis, who couldn't identify it at once, but, after consulting his bird-nest book, pronounced it to be that of a red-eyed vireo.

Oriole nest

So we had become acquainted with birds who nest near the ground and in nests in trees and bushes, but hole-nesters, other than our starlings, were something new. We were walking along a small road near our house one spring Sunday morning. We couldn't help noticing a big pile of wood chips at the base of a dead tree. The chips appeared to be four inches long, and looked like the work of a woodchopper. We had seen woodpeckers busily excavating ants from our trees, but the hole from which this debris came looked like a cavern.

A hole-nester

"Do you suppose that it could have been made by a pileated woodpecker?" I asked. Even as I spoke, Will pointed and called out, "There he is now!" And a huge, crowlike bird with black-and-white markings flew off at high speed. It couldn't have been anything but a pileated! Our day was made.

Not for long, though. When we proudly described our find to Rob, he laughed. "You've made the same old mistake! People always think a large rectangular hole with lots of chips below is a pileated's nest. You must know by now that birds don't advertise their nest sites. Pileated woodpeckers, when nest-building, will neatly drill out a smallish hole, usually triangular, and are careful not to leave any telltale chips around."

I must say it took a long time before we found a pileated's nest, so inconspicuous are they.

Why Do Birds Make Nests?

Birds need a safe place in which to lay eggs and raise their young. Nestmaking seems to be universal. Reptiles, fishes, some amphibians, and mammals use nests to keep their young together in one place to be cared for until they are old enough to care for themselves. Dinosaurs, which were ancestors of birds, probably laid their big eggs in shallow sun-warmed depressions and let nature take over. Some birds are still groundnesters, but others have evolved quite disparate methods of architecture, as we discovered on our walks.

Nests are built to discourage predators or to hide eggs from them, for birds need refuge from enemies at all times, but particularly during nesting season. How each species achieves this was our lesson that fall.

Incidentally, when the trees have lost their leaves—and even better, when they're capped with the first snowfall—the dark masses of the nests are easy to see. A collector is welcome to take nests then, because the birds won't use them again.

There seems to be an inverse relation between concealment and security. Accessible nests are carefully concealed and ground-nesters' eggs are well camouflaged. The ovenbird, a warbler, builds a nest that reminded the early settlers of their domed ovens, and it is so well hidden on the forest floor that we could scarcely see it. The meadowlark chooses a little scraped hollow or natural depression in which she assembles dried plant fibers, then makes a liner with

Nest security

finer grasses. Over all she erects a canopy of grass woven into the vegetation around it. And to make doubly sure that some predator won't find it, she often makes a tunnel of grass leading to the nest.

A number of species have survived with even less protection. The whippoorwill lays two eggs on a layer of oak leaves and lets it go at that, while a killdeer is satisfied with a shallow hollow lined with bits of gravel or bark or anything that is common to the immediate area. Other species need to have something more restraining to keep their eggs together. The tern in the sand or the bobolink in the hayfield can just reach out and draw a rolling egg back under her, but the swift in the chimney or the robin in a tree needs a cup to hold her eggs.

The cowbird   Then there is the cowbird. Nobody has much good to say about cowbirds. Most inattentive of mothers, not even bothering to make a nest, the female just flies about laying her six eggs, one a day, in others' nests. The foster parents, she hopes, will raise her young; and mostly they do. The danger is, of course, that the cowbird egg will hatch a little sooner and crowd or push the rightful small owners out of their own nests, or starve them to death. However, some disconcerted birds, such as the yellow warbler, will build another nest on top of the intrusive cowbird egg and start again. Robins and catbirds, wise creatures that they are, will simply roll the unwelcome egg over the edge, and good riddance! But we learned not to pass judgment too hastily on the female cowbird. For so many ages she lived mainly by following the buffalo in order to feed off the insects present with the roving herds, that she never had time to acquire proper nesting habits. Hastily laying an egg wherever she found a safe place, she had to leave it to hatch as best it could while she hurried after the buffalo. Man has succeeded in killing off the buffalo and turning its former habitat into farmland, and the cowbird, now ranging widely, uses the nests of other birds because she knows no other way to keep her eggs safe.

What is fascinating about nestmaking is that, on the average, each species prefers its own nesting habitat, using certain materials and dimensions that it knew as a juvenile. Furthermore, the first-year bird somehow knows how to buttress a foundation, how to gather the materials, how to weave them, how to line the interior—and all without a lesson. *Nest specialization*

In our city days, when we laughed at the birders, we charitably recognized that yes, it could conceivably be fun to distinguish one bird from another, but we never thought it would be just as fascinating to know where they nested and why, and what sort of nests they built, and why each species had evolved its instinct for what constituted a proper site.

Birds need nests for shelter. At first we hadn't connected birds with that word, since the one characteristic which most people think of in relation to a bird is its flight, that sense of freedom, all those associations with songs—"Oh, for the wings of a dove . . ." or, "the lark, the herald of the morn." We humans stand with feet planted in the clay and envy a bird its soaring into the sky. Shelter fits in with none of these images.

But now, though, Will and I had an inkling why a creature seemingly so free needs the proper shelter. And we hoped that we could provide such shelter, and so invite them to our home.

Catbird

Growing Up in a Nest

It's a wonder that any young birds survive to reach adulthood when one considers the length of brooding time, plus the number of days the nestlings have to be fed and watched over until they can fly. The fledgling time is particularly dangerous, since there exist so many creatures who depend on flesh for survival, and are on the alert for tasty eggs or a nestful of little birds.

Our Agnes was so fat and lazy that she wouldn't think of exerting herself by scrambling up a tree, even an easily climbed tree like our apples. But she did have a suitor in the neighbor's cat, and we heard reports of raccoons down the road. We knew there were snakes about because Katie started to pick up the hose one evening and it wriggled off.

Most of the birds that one hopes to attract are

perching birds—termed passerines, from the enormous and successful (in the sense of evolution) order of Passeriformes—which comprise three-fifths of all the birds in the world. Swallows, wrens, thrushes, sparrows, larks, warblers, flycatchers are only a few of the passerines. Most of these birds are alike in that they don't begin to incubate until the correct number of eggs has been laid. How does a bird know what constitutes the "correct" number of eggs? It seems to have something to do with the feel of the right number of eggs in the nest. One poor flicker, whose nest was robbed daily of an egg, laid seventy-one eggs in seventy-three days. I hope the scientist-turned-egg-thief finally let her keep a few, but the experiment did indicate that such birds are correctly called "indeterminate layers." In contrast, "determinate layers," like the plover and the sandpiper, lay four eggs, and will not lay more to fill the nest if any eggs are taken.

How many eggs

The number of eggs laid depends, too, on the rate of attrition each species must overcome. The more dangerous the circumstances in which a bird is typically reared, the more eggs it lays. The hummingbird for instance, lays only two eggs in its tiny and well-concealed nest; but a duck or pheasant whose eggs are laid on the ground and whose young must avoid all manner of dangers might have as many as fifteen in a clutch. Whatever the mechanism may be that allows a female passerine to know that she has laid the correct number of eggs and that she must start the brooding process, it ensures that the eggs hatch at the same time and have an equal start in life. On the other hand, the raptors, those birds like owls and hawks that depend on flesh for food, start to incubate from the day the first egg is laid, to make sure that their young hatch at intervals. Then, if times are hard and there's a scarcity of food, the oldest owl nestling may eat her little brother. I imagine that this is another instance of the survival of species, that at least the elder sister will have something to eat.

The first bird

The first flight of a true bird occurred on the day some 150 million years ago when a clumsy Archaeopteryx launched itself into the air to escape a hungry predator but fell into a swamp instead. For Archaeopteryx had feathers. We'd have trouble identifying this small dragon if he flew by today, but his fossilized remains clearly show feather imprints. In the millions of years since, birds have dropped their teeth, developed hollow bones, and acquired an enormously deep keel bone to which their flight muscles are attached. But they still keep the reptilian characteristic of encapsulating their embryos in shells, because a female bird cannot fly safely with a growing fetus within her. Only by having but one egg in an oviduct at a time can she escape her enemies. But this characteristic has its drawbacks, for it limits the number of eggs she can lay; and it requires absolutely that the nest be well concealed during the egg-laying process, which sometimes takes as long as ten days.

These fascinating bits and pieces of knowledge remained purely academic until the day when Will came into the kitchen with a cobweb attached to his collar, wanting to know where someone had put his tennis racquet. He'd left it in a cupboard in the ell wing where we stashed old boots and returnable bottles; no one had remembered seeing it. Taking off the sticky web he remarked that a bird was fluttering around in the bush just outside the ell window, and asked Katie please to pass him the guide on the shelf. We all tiptoed into the ell and peered stealthily out the window. There it was—and here came another! Not very exciting-looking, though. "Let's see, grey all over, but it's got a black cap. It has got to be a catbird. Yup, it's

him all right: see that reddish patch under his tail?"
Both birds, apparently ignoring our unenthusiastic
remarks on their coloring, hopped busily through the
branches of the old lilac just outside the window.

"What do you think?" I asked. "Do you suppose
they're getting ready to build a nest? The book says
they like dense cover, and this lilac is pretty dense."
The pair flew off and we returned to the kitchen to
hunt for Will's missing racquet. But next day, to our
delight, there they were again; and this time they appeared to be bringing bits of grasses and weed stalks in
their beaks. They were going to build in the lilac!

A catbird's nest

We really couldn't give an accurate account of what
they used and how they made the nest. We were so
new to the bird world that we didn't know what to
look for. Also, we couldn't just stand there to watch a
pair of catbirds wind weed stalks around one another.
We had to get on with the world's business. Or so we
thought, then, before we had begun to feel that
perhaps watching birds is also the world's business.

At any rate, the catbirds' business of building a catbird nest went on very satisfactorily. In five or six
days both catbirds had put together a bulky nest of
twigs, leaves, and grasses. There was a bit of newspaper too, and the cup appeared deep.

A plan occurred to all of us almost at the same time:
Why couldn't we see for ourselves how many eggs a
catbird laid and when she began to brood? It wouldn't
be hard, because they had thoughtfully established
themselves just outside, so we could look out at them
through the ell window. The murky window was
cleaned off for the first time in fifty years, I suppose,
and chairs placed by it. Any one of us who had a few
moments to spare would step as quietly as possible
across that creaky floor and see what the catbirds were
up to. It was surprising how many "free" moments we

found we had to spare for this activity. At first we were very careful and spoke in whispers, but the birds seemed to be unaware of us. The site in the lilac was perfect for us as well as for the nesting pair.

To the female catbird, three to five eggs under her feels right; she knows that is enough. Our bird felt that four was just right for her, and began to brood. We were separated by glass and by the void that exists between man and birds, so we couldn't tell when all this occurred in her brain and body, but one day we noticed that she was sitting quietly on the nest.

So the little catbird settled down to her stint while her mate, slim and trim in his grey, black-capped uniform, kept watch near by. And he was a good watchman, we found, for any time Agnes stalked by he set up a rapid series of nasal *hyeh-hyeh* mews that sounded very belligerent. At other times he perched on a branch of an apple tree, jerking his tail, and sang a rather pretty series of notes. The books say that he is an imitator like the mockingbird, but we didn't know enough to know whom he was supposed to be imitating. We liked it, though; and I suppose that Mrs. Catbird did too.

Mechanics of Brooding

Before we gave it much thought, we imagined that eggs would be warmed merely by being sat upon by the female. But when we learned that her feathers are insulation as well as aids to flight, we couldn't understand how heat got through the insulation to her eggs.

Rob Jarvis came to watch one day in our improvised bird blind and laughed when we admitted we were embarrassed to ask what seemed to be a simple-minded question. The answer *was* simple, he said.

The feathers on her breast had fallen out and the stored-up fat had disappeared, so the large number of blood vessels in that area now were available to raise the temperature of the skin. When we got sophisticated enough to be asked to a banding station, we were able to see a wood thrush whose bare breast was inflamed and hot to the touch. When a female alights on the nest and settles down with a sort of wiggle and a squirm, she is getting her eggs in contact with that featherless warm skin, called a "brood patch."

The "brood patch"

The first day our planned vigil went into operation was only a qualified success and engendered a bit of hard feeling. Will and Katie decided to take turns watching for a while in the morning to see if they could discover just what the pair was up to. In the time that the humans managed to sit still the female alone was on the nest, and we found that in the catbird family the male watches and guards but leaves to the female the boring part of raising the family. That, in general, seems to be the fate of female birds, for, in most species, the female sits for the twelve to fourteen days needed to hatch the eggs of songbirds.

Well, first Katie sat and then Will sat and neither of them had the patience that the catbird had, for as nearly as they could tell she stayed on the nest plumped-out for more than half an hour. Katie said she refused to donate another stint; Will said he wouldn't do hers too, and both left rather cross with one another. At that instant the female flew off. "There, now you've done it, Katie! I told you not to hiss so loud!" Will got a very angry look in reply. They came in to say that it was all over, the bird had flown off and all the eggs would get cold, and that it was each other's fault.

Ten minutes later I looked out and there she was, feathers fluffed, sitting quietly and calmly. We needn't have worried. Those short rest breaks make no difference at all. What really is dangerous is letting the eggs get, to use an old-fashioned expression, "addled." That's what happens when they become overexposed to heat in a nest that isn't well shaded from the sun, and fail to develop as they should.

What the amateurs did learn from their watching session was that the female got up and seemed to be arranging things about every seven minutes. And that's exactly what she was doing. She was turning the eggs so that they got warmed on all sides equally. You know how it is with an egg that is cooked in not enough water—it's all squishy in the underdone part.

For about two weeks the mother catbird sat and turned and turned and sat, keeping the eggs at a temperature of about 90 degrees Fahrenheit. We tried to imagine what was happening inside those fragile shells. We knew that the embryos had grown quickly; that in fact they had started to develop even before the eggs had left the mother's body. Development had stopped temporarily when they were laid, but had started up again when she started to brood. The yolk, which had almost filled the shell at first, soon had blood vessels radiating nourishment to the small embryo. Not long thereafter, the yolk had been almost totally absorbed. Two days before they hatched, the unborn chicks had begun to breathe, using the air in the blunt end of the shell and obtaining more oxygen through the now porous shell, whose lime had been incorporated in the tiny bones.

Inside the egg

The Hatching

Did the parents know it was time for their family to appear? Could they hear faint cheeping messages from within that minuscule world? Did a sense of claustrophobia inform the unborn that it was time to free themselves from their confining prison?

On the natal morning one of us, going through the ell to the kitchen, glanced out the "observation window" (as we grandly called it) and saw in the nest a naked little head encrusted with sticky bits of shell. Our own breakfast eggs were left cooling in the cups as we all gathered to watch an egg begin to separate around in the middle, exposing a reddish, crumpled bit of skin.

The first chick was struggling to free its wing and was so obviously making hard work of it that we wanted to rush outside and help. We wanted to see that bird make its journey from his tiny safe world to the endless universe that stretched forever before him. Oh, dear! We locked a meowing Agnes in the screened porch and left the birds to their job of getting themselves into the world.

At six o'clock we tiptoed out to the window, feeling like grandparents on a first visit to a hospital nursery. There was Mamma sitting plumped-out as before, but did we detect a smug look on her bright-eyed face? As if knowing that we were anxious to see the newborn, she flew off the nest. By standing on our toes we could just barely see into the cup. We were aghast. Four minute lumps of rumpled pink flesh attached to oversized bare heads, huge swollen eyelids . . . Beauty is in the eye of the beholder, they say. As we watched, she returned, jiggled the nest when she alighted on it, and at once four enormous yellow maws popped open. As she proceeded to stuff bits of a green caterpillar into each mouth in turn, the yellow openings closed and the heads sank down into the nest.

Unlovely hatchlings

"Well, you'd never know that those things would turn out to be jaunty catbirds, would you?" Will said.

We could see that Katie was a bit upset at what the birds had hatched. And I must admit that we adults didn't think much of the hatchlings either.

That night Rob came to see the nursery and over a cup of coffee gave us a blow-by-blow account of what had gone on in the delivery room that morning.

A day after the unborn bird "wakes up" by starting to breathe, it begins to rub its egg tooth (a reminder that its cousin is a snake, for snakes also have an egg tooth) against the shell. For about four hours it rubs away with that temporary bony protuberance on the upper beak and finally pips the shell. But that isn't enough, for it has to repeat this procedure until there are five or six star-shaped holes halfway around the largest part of the egg, the infant shifting its position within the shell for each new hole. While this wearisome process is taking place the yolk sac, which has nourished the baby, is still hanging outside its body. Just as the shell is about to be burst in two by the struggling infant, the last of the sac is pulled inside the stomach and the opening closes. The shell breaks apart, the little morsel lies among the debris, exhausted—but out in the world.

We three sat gaping in wonder. A miracle had occurred in our lilac bush.

It seemed to us that the parents turned themselves into feeding machines from the moment the babies had hatched. Not quite, though, for hatchlings at first are too tired by their birth struggle to eat anything the parent might offer. For the first few hours of life they are sustained by the last of the yolk so recently absorbed. After that the parents appear never to have a moment's rest. Someone has had the patience to record the number of visits one set of phoebe parents made to feed their young. It came to the astonishing number of 845 in one day! Birds have been known actually to die of overwork.

How Birds Feed

For the first four days the young catbirds' eyes were closed, but they knew that a nest-jiggle meant food, so the yellow pouches opened automatically. The parent probed down into each cavity in turn, its bill triggering a swallowing response in the baby, whose bright-colored gullet is thought to elicit from the parents an impulse to feed the infant.

After the chicks' eyes open, a more sophisticated approach to the world is developed. Jiggles without a parent in sight mean enemies, so down go the heads and the bright yellow mouths are kept closed. Now the parents wait until they are seen, which in turn makes the nestlings cry; then the feeding process is resumed. The feeding cry is very useful later in enabling parents to find fledglings that have strayed.

It's hard to imagine that anything so tiny as those four young catbirds could hold all the thousands of *Diet* insects, soft grubs, and caterpillars that were stuffed down their throats; each ate an amount almost equal to its own weight every day. Even babies that will grow up to become seed-eaters subsist on a diet of insects, which are high in protein and contain the water the infants need.

It was here that we came across the term "altricial," from the Latin for "nurse." Catbirds are altricial birds. They have to be nursed. They emerge from their tiny shells in twelve days, naked, blind, and helpless. But nature has seen to it that they are programmed to gain weight at an enormous rate with the high-protein diet *Altricial and* their parents provide. *precocial species*

The opposite of altricial is "precocial," also from the Latin, meaning that almost at once, upon hatching, the babies can feed themselves and scuttle for safety under their mother's wings. Loons, duck, and pheasant, to name some precocial birds, lay large roomy eggs in which their young can take time to grow strong legs, thick down, and strong beaks. But birds can't have it both ways. The mother of precocial young has them under her care a lot longer. Goslings don't fly for six or seven weeks; a meadowlark will leave its nest in twelve days.

Our little brood, looking very altricial indeed, grew so fast that we didn't see how they all fitted in the nest. It resembled a basket with four ungainly knobs covered with wild tufts of down, to which were attached huge yellow mouths. To add to the generally unattractive scene, the babies almost constantly complained in an unmusical squawk.

In about seven days the birds had begun to lose their naked repulsive look, with feathers pushing out of casings in the skin. In ten days the chicks actually began to look like birds.

All this time the parents had been busy, at first keeping them warm, disposing of the discarded shells so that predators wouldn't be attracted to the nest site, and in the housekeeping job of keeping the nest clean. The nestlings eliminate into fecal sacs which are then carried off by their parents. In this manner the nest is kept tidy and the ground around is not covered by a lot of droppings that would serve to alert enemies. And on top of all this the adults had the endless task of finding food for themselves and their children.

Soon the catbird chicks were approaching the most dangerous stage of their lives, nest-leaving. Under-feathered, unwary fledglings fall prey to all the predators who are forever on the lookout for a meal.

First Flight

We missed the great day of nest-leaving, alas. But the previous day we noticed a good deal of activity in the nest. The parents swooped by in short passes, uttering cheeps and calls. The babies stretched and beat their wings, and one brave little soul scrambled to the edge of the nest, lost his balance, and saved himself only by frantic beatings.

When we looked out the next evening, the nest was empty. We felt like parents whose children had left home. The catbird children were about, though, hidden from us and other beings not so well disposed. The young birds were separated and warned to keep quiet, not to squawk, for silence is nature's greatest protection. The parents flew about in the general area, not concentrating their movements but listening for the offsprings' muted food cries.

Later we learned the pattern of development after nest-leaving. Usually for a few days, the tail and wing feathers are growing. Then the flying lessons are begun, two weeks or so of muscle-building and confidence and learning the refinements of flight. Once the young are mobile, the family comes together again to be schooled for a week in the gathering of food and how to avoid enemies. Then they are on their own. And most of them don't make it. Ornithologists in the United States estimate that two-thirds of the birds hatched each year die before that year is out.

Nest-leaving

It was an anxious time for all of us. The cat was let out only for short strolls, since we couldn't be sure that her slothful nature would withstand the sight of fat young catbirds in the grass, and we shooed away neighboring animals. The birds were worn to a frazzle keeping an eye on the children and watching out for the hungry others who also have to exist. But there were moments of fun, particularly on one Sunday afternoon when we watched a father robin give a lesson to his young son on how to hop and on how to stop and listen for worms (we didn't know until later that

Worm-catching lessons

robins don't listen). The youngster was almost as large as his parent but lacked the length of tail and wing feathers; his head still had the untidy look of adolescence. He complained constantly in a harsh voice, losing sight of his father and hopping frantically to catch up. The lesson didn't appear to go too well, for the father finally had to poke worms at him. We could almost imagine him saying to himself that he just didn't see how the younger generation could be so dull.

But the best incident of all happened the next day. Visiting cousins came for the afternoon, bringing with them their half-grown and very amiable setter, Albert. Albert exhibited exemplary dog manners and sat quietly in the garden enjoying country smells. The warm air was light, the lawn and garden looked under control, and we were happily exchanging family gossip. But almost overhead a bluebird family was undergoing a crisis. We became aware of that as the agitated parents' instructions grew louder than our voices. What probably happened was that, out of bravado, a youngster flew off in the direction of our apple trees and, to his surprise, found a company of human beings below. He wasn't terribly worried, but his parents were upset. They loudly urged him to fly straight away to safety. The scolding finally grew so loud that we stopped talking and looked up into the branches of the tree overhead just in time to see the offending young bluebird launch himself off. Wings flailing, looking desperately around—for it was apparent that his ambitions were stronger than his muscles—he spied the noble domed head of Albert—and lit upon it. For almost half a minute we sat like stone statues; even the aghast parents uttered not a squeak. The baby panted on his new platform and Albert, aware that something had happened to his head, rolled his eyes upward in a classic pose that has never left our memories.

Our catbird family may have raised another family. A number of the perching birds do. We know that they didn't return to the old nest, because unseen mites and parasites infest old nests.

But we do know about the end of July the evening concerts gradually ceased; and in those lovely long summer twilights we no longer heard the songs of the orioles, bluebirds, robins, and wood thrushes, sounding like a sonata for flutes. The birds were worn out by the constant attention to their offspring. Their feathers were frazzled and frayed by the unending search for food. They were content to rest for the remainder of the summer, gathering strength for the long trip south in the fall. And for those who stayed behind to face the fight for survival during the months of freezing weather, this was a resting period too.

Preparing for migration

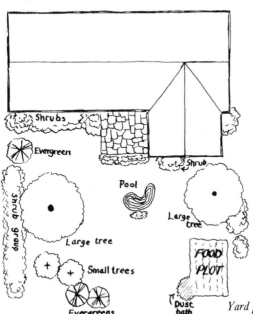

Yard plan showing relative positions of water, cover, feed

Cedar waxwing

Some Birds Would Rather Eat Raspberries

Our four young catbirds were lucky enough, we hoped, to reach adolescence unscathed. Lucky, because the parents had chosen the correct nest site to provide plenty of concealing cover. Important, too, was that the area had available lots of their favorite food: insects, caterpillars, and cutworms. What a quantity of these squashy but delectable offerings had been brought by the parents to the nest! The unfortunate worm munching away on our cabbage plants stood little chance against the catbirds' sharp eyes and tweezerlike bills. Somehow the pair knew that our lawn, garden, and shrubs afforded just the food their prospective children would need. If the four fledglings were fortunate, some or all would live to be parents themselves.

But catbirds weren't the only birds nesting on our place. What about the cedar waxwing? What did he and his family prefer to eat? And the bluebird, the hummingbird, the chickadees, and the flycatcher we had seen flying about: why did they, too, live and raise their families around us?

Insect eater

We had learned that birds look for spots in which their nests will have cover, and that encouraging shrubs and trees to provide shelter and nest foundations will entice birds to accept one's welcome to live near by.

But food must be available, as well. To forget it would be like offering to put up a friend but overlooking the bread and wine.

Did all these birds like the same food? Well, to start with the most obvious example, the hummingbird. He couldn't fly with even a cutworm in his beak; and he didn't have the catbird's tweezers with which to tweak a cutworm from a leaf, for, instead, his bill was like a drinking straw. And the flycatcher seems to snap up his prey, while the robin yanks.

It became quite clear that not only did the birds like dissimilar food, they couldn't gather others' choice tidbits.

A macabre mobile of bird skulls in a natural history museum showed the reason for this difference explicitly. Each skull was as different as—well, as a horse is from a cat. They were alike only in that each one had a beak, eye sockets, and was made of calcium. A grosbeak's (its name is appropriate) round bony skull with two yellow cones forming the bill, balanced a slowly revolving heron's skull. The short nutcracking bill of the grosbeak was in complete contrast to the frog-

Seed eater

*Smaller seed
eater*

piercing rapier of the heron. It was readily apparent that neither could eat the food favored by the other. We, who can so effortlessly get to the supermarket and buy freeze-dried peas or canned octopus tentacles, overlook the evolutionary process that birds have gone through. Their "arms" and "hands" are used for flying. In order to get their food they have to use their bills as tweezers, swords, nippers, nutcrackers. We, who would invite birds to our home, have difficulty realizing the long process of evolution which has equipped each species to find, pick up, and consume only a certain kind of food. We must help make it available to those whom we wish to welcome.

It seemed to us before we issued any invitations for dinner that it was well to know the food likes and dislikes of those invited. How embarrassing to set before a guest a carefully prepared steak tartare only to find the guest a dedicated vegetarian!

The very first thing we learned was that the majority of songbirds in our garden were seed-eaters. With knowledge came a bit of geological lore. In fact, it's astounding how much we learned without knowing we were doing so, all through becoming interested in that very first blackbird. Smatterings to be sure, but we were led to think about plants and their interrelation with birds; about the seasons, biology, evolution, and even something about stars and migration. And to our surprise and amazement, for the first time, Latin made a bit of sense in naming the orders and genera of birds!

Flesh eater

But back to the geology lesson. Birds have been about in one form or another for at least 150 million years, although we'd not recognize as a bird one of those flying dinosaurs. That's what all birds, even the delicate hummingbird, are descended from, much as we may not like to think so.

A mere 13 million years ago during the Miocene Period the earth was drained of many seas and swamps and marshes, and as the land dried out, vast expanses of veldts, steppes, and prairies rolled to endless horizons. Grasses and their seed flourished, and with them evolved birds who could take advantage of this *Seed eaters* new but easily gathered food. The bills of these seed-eaters became stout, strong mandibles that could crack the shells of the seeds and extract the kernel. The great proliferation of seed-eaters is an example of Darwin's theory that natural selection enabled such creatures to develop a bill that could utilize the vast amounts of seed produced by that particular geologic age. Many evolutionists regard the seed-eaters as the most recently evolved birds; particularly the finches and buntings, whose conical bills are especially efficient in seed-cracking.

Seed-eaters are part of the Passeriformes order, which, as we have seen, comprises sixty percent of all the birds in the world. It was natural, then, that seed-eaters were the majority of birds on our place.

Seeds were almost too easy for our property to produce. Everything around us was putting out seeds like crazy. The pair of goldfinches were delighted with the down from our dandelions and thistles with which they line their nests and whose seeds they feed their young. Our neighbor wasn't so happy. Will muttered that if the thistle was good enough to be the symbol of Scotland, it should be good enough for Mr. Farwell.

With the seed-eaters apparently taken care of, we began to wonder about those birds who liked berries and fruits. What about the cedar waxwings, robins, myrtle warblers, thrashers, to name only a few who looked for food other than seeds? Except for the apples there didn't seem to be many plants on our place that

would be inviting to berry-eaters and that would provide emergency food for wintering birds. Plants mean
planting. Planting important things like trees and
shrubs. It sounded like money and hard work. We
thought we'd better know what we were about.

The first thing, obviously, was to find out just what
sort of birds came here to nest or to winter over. As

Wintering birds   Will said, it was no use to go ahead and put in plants
for birds that were seen only a thousand miles away, or
try to invite a bird that likes spruce seeds in the
mountains and wouldn't think of coming to our suburban plot. At the same time, we should keep in
mind the sort of planting that would give nesting birds
good nest foundations and protective cover.

I will admit that, although gathering information
took time and some effort, this chapter in our bird
adventure was one of the most entertaining. I suppose
we were fortunate in trying to dig it out for ourselves,
because in doing so we became acquainted with our
new social environment.

Every community harbors at least one kindly expert, people who are founts of knowledge on birds in
the area and seem always eager to help with questions
and to impart their bird lore. In fact, we found all
birders happy to share their enthusiasm and information with us, neophytes though we were.

Another source was the weekly newspaper, unlikely as this may seem to a city dweller. On any suburban or rural paper there's sure to be a corre-
spondent who's a bird-lover, and who usually has a
note or a column about the birds at her feeder or
nesting on her place. Interspersed with news of village
visits, broken bones, and church alliance meetings,
there will be mention of the warbler in her rosebush or
a purple finch at the feeder. We gained a lot of solid
knowledge of birds' eating and nesting habits simply
by reading our local *Trumpet*.

Trips to the natural history museums in the city and consultation with the state Audubon Society helped to confirm the knowledge gathered locally.

When we had compiled what we considered to be adequate lists we found that we had not only learned a lot about birds but that our knowledge of our community had grown. Best of all, we had made friends! And we were pretty sure we weren't going to make the mistake of looking for a Western meadowlark in an Eastern suburb. Or planting the wrong sort of bush for a cedar waxwing to collect food from.

Armed with our lists we went to see our favorite oracle, Rob Jarvis, to ask what trees and shrubs we should plant to make up for our deficiency in providing nesting and feeding areas.

"Have you got landscape plans laid out yet?" We hadn't thought of that, we answered. "Well, don't go near a nurseryman or even think of planting anything until you've made a long-range plan of what you want your place to look like five years from now and twenty years from now." He looked at our fallen faces. "It's not really hard. Don't be upset by the long-term idea. I know that you can't be sure you'll be here twenty years from now, but consider how much more valuable your place will be if you do have to move if it's well planted. And chances are that you'll be right here to enjoy it."

How to Plan For Birds

Here are his suggestions. We had our front lawn and space on either side of the house and a good area in back, and behind that the wet place where the redwings were. We should go home and pace off the boundary around our place; no need to use a measuring tape: just figure Will's stride (probably three feet if he used a long one). Then we should plot out where all the existing trees and buildings were. If we wanted to be quite accurate, we could use a 12-inch ruler and let each of the marks represent a foot.

Landscaping for birds

When we had gotten it all on paper, we should sit down with one another at different windows and on the back porch, trying to figure out what we'd like to see there in a few years' time. We must keep in mind that the lot next to us probably would be sold, and we might want to screen it out. Where would we want the flower garden to be and how far did we want to walk to get a head of lettuce from the vegetable garden? Block out our property, frame it, to have both open and massed effects. All this planning was for our benefit, because we'd be the ones who would live there and pay for it.

We should think how it would look in summer and winter, and this meant we'd want both evergreen and deciduous plants When, by our own efforts or with help from a professional landscaper or after consulting ready-made plans, we had done all these things, then—and only then—we could start to find out what sorts of trees and bushes to plant that would invite birds. The thing to remember was that birds must have cover, water, and food.

"And for heaven's sakes," Rob warned us, "don't fuss about the exact tree or shrub until you've thought through what you want to see around you. Be sure. It's a lot easier to erase a mark on a paper than it is to move a tree."

Sources of information

Rob's was probably the best advice we'd gotten since we moved from the city. It took time and thought, but finally we were ready to ask what trees and plants could be put in that would be inviting and sustaining for birds. Audubon Societies, natural history centers, local experts were our sources, and we found that we'd better be quite specific in knowing the particular likes and dislikes of our local birds, for in the county below us the same species preferred quite a different berry from the ones grown locally. Rob warned us not to overlook a source easily available, the agronomist at our county Extension Service. "Why, there's all sorts of information there. Use it; you've paid for it with your taxes. He's got pamphlets on everything on earth from bladderworms in sheep to what causes screaming fits in minks."

We found that the County Agent was also ready with information more immediate and practical concerning our problems. I admit I felt a bit frivolous in asking his help in enticing birds to our house, but if he smiled he did it inwardly.

From the long list of suggestions we had compiled from our sources he picked out trees and shrubs that did well in our area, and he gave us the name of a nurseryman he considered reputable. And we shouldn't overlook the possibilities of getting our own small trees and shrubs from friends in the country or from farmers. We'd save lots of money But we shouldn't forget to ask permission first.

As we were leaving he reminded us to take pamphlets on digging proper holes for planting, on fertilizing, watering, and pruning. All the material was filled with stern admonitions to do the job correctly. Would bowed shoulder, digger's elbow, and bursitis be the result? Would all this effort and fuss be worth it?

The man we went to on the agent's suggestion did away with our city-bred fears. Calm and sure in his movements from years of supervising the estates of old-time residents, he seemed to let his hands move independently in their task of potting seedlings, We made it plain that we envisioned starting slowly in our plan for planting to invite birds and that furthermore we were not sure that we could follow the grim instructions in the pamphlets. He listened as he sifted potting soil and said only, "I'll be over." Which he was, the next week.

He smiled at the apple trees, and at our starling-thwarters stuffed in the holes. "Aren't many old orchards like these anymore. Those Baldwins were great keepers. And the bluebirds used to love the holes in them until the starlings drove them out."

First plantings

After our walk of inspection and over a cup of tea and a thorough study of our plans, he proposed to start us off by helping us plant two mulberries in the rich soil behind the barn. "Two together so they'll be male and female to be sure that the female will bear. Their berries are dreadful squashy and get on ladies' shoes, but the birds do love them. If you ever put in raspberry or strawberry beds, the mulberries will attract the birds away from them."

We felt that two mulberries were within our budget. And if we were willing to dig the holes, he would show where the digging would be boulder-free, and he would plant the trees. The digging wasn't really too bad, for by some diviner's sense he picked places that were boulderless and rootless.

He arrived in his battered pickup, our two little trees looking pitifully spindly, their roots bound up in burlap balls lying on a well-rotted pile of cow manure. Where he had gotten manure in our sanitized town, we couldn't imagine. The process of planting, which appeared so laborious and tricky and fraught with disaster if not done exactly right, was done easily with our latter-day Johnny Appleseed in command. His instructions about watering, fertilizing, and pruning actually made sense. We felt much like a young couple with a newborn baby when a comfortable grandmother gives common-sense advice.

Our two tiny mulberries took root with hardly a dropped leaf. Today they are full grown and feeding countless birds. So much for bursitis and digger's elbow.

As for others of the songbird species who preferred insects and such, well, they had to make do with the delectable morsels found under leaves and behind cracks in bark. We couldn't do much to supply them with such food; it was up to them. However, there does seem to be enough to go around. Insects which have found a niche in just about every part of the globe can't escape the searching birds. For every bug that lives under a leaf or buzzes about, there is a bird like the warbler, or that flying acrobat, the swallow, or that remorseless bark-prober, the nuthatch. It's often claimed that if birds didn't exist, we'd be overwhelmed by insects. While this is an exaggeration, since the bird population must also be kept in control, it is true that where man has inadvertently killed off birds, the insects have increased like Pharaoh's plague of locusts.

Providing for insect eaters

Out planting plan has now been carried through, but it has some years to go before the big trees reach their full height. The hedges, shrubs, and what small ornamental trees we could afford are doing nicely. We have a homemade pool with lawn about it and a garden that pleases us as well as the birds. The choice of nesting sites has been greatly increased and we have provided a variety of food for the birds who have accepted our invitation to live with us. We have done this with a minimum of money expended because we knew what we wanted and what was possible for our particular area.

People with old places in the country with wildly overgrown land, or who have bought a tract house in a development that looks like a geological disaster, or the dwellers deep in the city—all can issue an invitation to birds and have it accepted.

Plants That Please Us
and the Birds

It's fifteen years now since we planted those mulberries in hope and faith. Last Sunday Will and I had breakfast under the apple trees and watched a hummingbird hover over a nicotiana in the garden. A goldfinch in its wavering flight appeared from our rough patch behind the old barn where we had let some thistles go to seed. From the wet spot Mrs. Robin was busy carrying mud plaster for her second nest. The distant descendants of the first red-winged blackbird were bringing up their children in the little marsh in back of the house. It was still not filled in and nothing obnoxious had ever emerged from it that we knew of. The blackbirds were doing a fine job of keeping the bug population down.

We had song sparrows, phoebes, cardinals, cedar waxwings, kingbirds, barn swallows, flickers, orioles, wood thrushes. They lived with us or near by, but were attracted to our bushes and gardens for their food. In the winter we kept goldfinches, chickadees, nuthatches, purple finches, hairy woodpeckers, juncos, evening grosbeaks, and, of course, jays, supplied with food and shelter. The very first thing we do on coming downstairs in the morning is to look out on our snowy lawn and see who has appeared for breakfast. In the bushy evergreens, the summer visitors nest or retreat from the hot sun, while in the winter the hardy stay-overs huddle together on their protective branches.

In planning for wild birds, the most important single thing to keep in mind is to furnish a variety of food and cover. It ensures that you will be able to welcome a variety of birds.

The easiest way to make sure you've done this is to provide what is known as the "edge effect." The edge effect is a combination of lawns, shrubbery, seedy corner, and trees, both deciduous and evergreen. It is open space, with some water available and food-bearing plants with cover near by. Birds will be invited both to nest and to feed on your property. *The "edge effect"*

You'll notice as you become more learned in bird ways that it's no use looking for most of the songbirds in a deep mature forest. They just aren't there, for such a habitat doesn't provide them with much of the cover or food that they require. The wise birder goes to look for them at the edge of such a wood, where it gives way to fields by way of bushes and low shrubs. During the time of nesting many birds are of low mobility and they are attracted to places where food, cover, and water are within reach.

The large expanses of rather sterile lawns, brought

about by the ubiquitous little tractor, are of little use to any but a robin. Robins are fine with smooth lawns—but what about the other species you wish to welcome? So break up lawns by creating the edge effect with gardens, shrubs, vines, and trees.

Open space   We started our planning by considering the already established lawn in back as the center around which we would plan our bird sanctuary. We kept two of the old trees to furnish shade and to use as a vantage spot from which to see what was going on about us. At the sides, to screen out the proposed houses still to be built on the vacant lots next to us, we planted blackberry with hawthorn behind it. To provide a background to the hawthorn, we put in red cedars. In the beginning we *Cover*   had planted the screening bushes and trees rather closer than is commonly advised, with the hopes that we would soon have something to provide good cover for the birds and which would shelter us from the house next door. We did this knowing that we might have to thin them out later.

Flower garden   In back, the flower garden, already there, was re-planted to include things that both the seed-eaters and the hummingbirds like. Beyond, red osiers, winter-berry, and autumn olive protected the vegetable sec-tion. Flowering crab and dogwood were located where they could float above the lower shrubs. In the rear, to provide a massive background, were planted a clump *Larger trees*   of white pines. In the Northern states, evergreens like spruce, pine, hemlock, and cedar are a must for shel-ter both winter and summer. Be sure you provide for them when you plan.

In the opposite corner red maples are now reaching upwards, making a good contrast to the pines al-though they have been in only fifteen years. We were fortunate in inheriting some large trees, but if you have to start from scratch a good plan will work wonders in even a few years. The very first step of starting a lawn and putting in a flower garden—even if it is annuals to start with—and planting a few of the proposed shrubs, will have an almost immediate effect. Smaller ornamental trees will transform a place in five years. In ten years a maple and a pine will have grown to a respectable twenty feet. With today's fashion for smaller one-story houses, perhaps large trees may be a trifle overwhelming.

Natural Food for Birds

At the rear of the old barn was our rough spot, where we grew patches of bird feed. And here the compost heap slowly did its work.

Seed-eaters appreciated the ripening grass heads in the rough spot, and you'll find, as we did, that by simply avoiding exertion and not mowing in a certain wild plot you've attracted some very desirable bird tenants. Rose-breasted grosbeaks, juncos, buntings, and those brilliant, favorite cardinals are all seed-eaters. With luck you may have them nesting on your place.

Later, we were told that our rough spot would be more productive if we divided it into plots or strips, and dug or plowed one strip each year so that the strips would be in various states of cultivation, offering differing vegetation for a variety of birds.

A more ambitious plan would be to seed down small plots to sunflowers, millet, and rye for the seed-eaters. These plots could be as large as a quarter-acre or as small as 10 square feet.

Even in the flower garden the seed-eaters can be helped if you're not being too zealous in clipping off the dead heads. Let some ripen in the pods; a few,

"Wild" foods

perhaps in the rear of the border, aren't going to spoil the effect of the garden. Those drying heads may just make the difference in whether a bird pair considers responding to your welcome.

Don't be too neat about cleaning up around the edges. Will got into a frenzy of tidiness one summer and laid low a large frowzy patch of jewelweed. Then he wondered why the hummingbird wasn't buzzing around us as usual. It was pointed out by a very cross Katie that he'd just destroyed one of the things that had attracted them to our place.

Restrained Trimming and Natural Shelter

I well remember another lesson we got one day early in our country life from dear old Rob Jarvis. We were trying to reduce our shaggy, leggy overgrown privet hedge to some sort of respectability. It was one of the first hot days. We took turns and clipped until our arms ached—even Katie was pressed into service. That hedge seemed to stretch on before us forever. Just as we were beginning to curse the very idea of a hedge, Rob drove slowly by, looking things over. We waved, hoping he would stop. He pulled over and sat looking at our efforts. Then a smile lightened his somber face, which resembled an ancient but benevolent eagle's. "I've got good news for you. You don't have to work so hard on that pesky hedge. Supposing you were suddenly turned into a little bird and hard on your heels was a goshawk. You'd spy that hedge and dive into it, safe. But a hedge that's all neat and tidy and close-clipped, well, it's goodbye little bird, and a good meal for Mr. Goshawk. Birds can't get into a dense hedge. So why don't you all go and have a glass of iced tea? In fact, I'll join you."

Now the hedge has achieved a degree of respectability in keeping with our neighborhood, in that its wildest shoots have been restrained. It looks tidy, but it will never resemble those fat yew pillows that all too many suburban property owners have set up against their houses, or be like those fortresslike green barriers dividing one lawn from another. Nevertheless, it satisfies birds that dwell in low bushes and it offers shelter and protection. *Hedges for shelter*

Birds must be able to move freely inside. Prolonged trimming of ornamental planting produces a multiplicity of tiny twiglets. But after all isn't it rather a relief to know that you don't have to have the smoothest hedges in the world? What a good excuse not to have to spend those long, boring hours clipping away when a good game of tennis is more fun, and better for you! A hedge thickly grown with lots of little branchlets inside may be a death trap for an unwary bird who builds a nest therein, because the neighborhood cat and all the other ground predators will have easy access to the nest, and the bird herself will have difficulty escaping through such dense growth.

You can plant hedges like rugosa rose and barberry, which grow quickly, furnishing food and cover that even the most hardy predator hesitates to penetrate. These plants can be an effective screen for compost heaps or garbage cans. Other small and fast-growing screens are autumn olive, bush honeysuckle, and high-bush cranberry.

One of the most ingenious ideas we've heard of is letting birds do your planting. In the fall, plow a strip where you wish to establish a bird-inviting hedgerow, set up posts, string wire between them—and then sit back and let the birds do the work of seeding the plot. Wade Hamor, biologist for the United States Soil Conservation Service, whose brilliant idea this is, claims that the fruit-eaters, the cardinals and cedar waxwings and robins, to name only a few, will light on your inviting roost and drop their favorite berry seeds. Before you know it you may have a dogwood, wild cherry, blackberry, or mulberry hedgerow.

Keep in mind that plants that furnish food for birds will not be the ones in which they nest. No self-respecting bird will build a nest in a tree or shrub where every bird neighbor in the area will come to get food. There must be planting that will provide both. That is why variety is stressed over and over.

Around and through our place we made paths that led people to where we wanted them to go and which kept them from straying into places sacred to birds.

Providing Nesting Places

In all our planning we were careful to keep in mind that we wanted birds to live with us, actually to nest on our property. When they seem to be flying about in a careless manner, they are really cruising about looking for the right combination of angle, branch support, and leafy cover in which to start their nest foundation. Until we went out one day early in our planning to look at what our place offered to tree-nesting birds, and tried to imagine we were birds looking it over for possibilities, we never realized how really few places we provided. (Since trees don't grow overnight, we overcame the lack of good sites by putting in the sorts of nesting boxes described in Chapter 12.)

First comes the problem of finding a niche or crotch that isn't too wide or too narrow. It's estimated, we read, that birds like an angle of 70 degrees. They seem to know just about what angle will hold the first bits of straw or twigs they put down. When a correctly angled crotch is found, a serious bird couple will require that it have enough branches to support the cup of the nest; but—and this is most important—the site cannot be near the trunk or near any largish branches up which four-footed creatures can travel. We realized that, if we wanted birds to nest, we would have to provide trees and shrubs that would fill the requirements of birds who like to nest high up, such as a cerulean warbler who likes its nest to be about thirty to forty feet up in a deciduous tree. A solitary vireo, on the other hand, prefers an evergreen with a branch only fifteen feet above the ground. Its cousin, the red-eyed vireo, likes a shrub with a good strong fork from which to hang its deep cup.

Don't forget that many birds, from chickadees to woodpeckers, will come and live with you if you have a dead tree around. Don't be too quick to cut it down if it presents no danger. Besides furnishing nesting holes, such a tree harbors all sorts of insects that nuthatches, creepers, and woodpeckers are looking for; and when the tree finally falls, it fosters other life that in turn attracts birds. Further, all species seem to relish a chance to sit in the sun, much as we do in spring and fall. And last, the topmost limbs of a dead tree make a fine perching place to look things over and keep an eye out for enemies. Think of all this when you consider taking down that tree.

Dead trees

If you leave some chokecherries to fruit, they'll be messy, but they will attract the robins away from your prized raspberries.

The space you have to work with may be greatly expanded by getting your neighbors to go in with you in inviting the birds and wildlife. In fact, you could end up by having a wildlife preserve in your combined backyards. Expenses, too, can be shared in planting and in supplying food in the winter months.

So far I have been discussing plans for those who are country dwellers or suburbanites. But city folks also may issue invitations to birds. A feeder outside a window, a shallow pan of water on a fire escape with a potted plant may be just the dash of green in a wilderness of bricks and concrete that attracts the eye of a weary migrant.

Some Ideas for Trees, Shrubs, and Annuals

In considering the following suggestions remember that the trees and plants listed are general, and not necessarily specific to the area under which they're grouped. A bayberry listed for the Northeast may do beautifully on Cape Cod but would quickly succumb to Vermont's icy winters. Check with your County Agent or favorite nurseryman on what is hardy in your particular neck of the woods.

Here are some trees that certain birds like:

Beech   Bluejay, towhee, titmouse, cardinal.

Black cherry   Robin, towhee, mockingbird, vireo, flicker, finch.

Flowering dogwood   Kingbird, waxwing, cardinal, catbird, brown thrasher, woodpecker, purple finch, vireo, robin, towhee, bluebird.

Hackberry (or *Nettle Tree* or *Sugarberry*)   Brown thrasher, robin, mockingbird, cardinal, flicker, bluebird.

Holly   Bluebird, catbird, waxwing, brown thrasher, flicker, thrush, robin, mockingbird.

Mountain ash   Cedar waxwing, catbird, robin, flicker.

Mulberry   Thrush, cuckoo, waxwing, warbler, vireo, oriole, cardinal.

Oak   Grackle, bluejay, woodpecker, crow, nuthatch, brown thrasher, titmouse.

Pine Nuthatch, chickadee, warbler, grosbeak, titmouse, brown thrasher, bluejay.

Red cedar Sparrow, bluebird, flicker, robin, purple finch, mockingbird, cardinal.

Sassafras Catbird, robin, flicker, vireo, towhee.

Shadbush (or *Juneberry* or *Serviceberry*) Cardinal, bluebird, flicker, catbird, thrush, scarlet tanager.

Sour gum Purple finch, waxwing, bluebird, towhee, robin, flicker, brown thrasher.

Here are some shrubs:

Bayberry Catbird, chipping sparrow, junco, thrush, song sparrow.

Blackberry Oriole, sparrow, vireo, woodpecker, towhee, thrush, catbird.

Blueberry Titmouse, robin, chickadee, cardinal, waxwing, phoebe, cardinal.

Elderberry Indigo bunting, woodpecker, chat, kinglet, phoebe, towhee, cardinal.

Pokeberry Cardinal, bluebird, robin, mourning dove, flicker, catbird, towhee.

Privet Catbird, waxwing, thrasher, robin, mockingbird.

Pyracantha Waxwing, brown thrasher, mockingbird, robin, bluebird, finch.

Snowberry Grosbeak, bobwhite, thrush, robin, cedar waxwing.

Spicebush Catbird, cardinal, robin, vireo.

Viburnum Finch, bluebird, thrush, waxwing, flicker, robin.

The following are commonly cultivated annuals. Because they belong to the same group of wild plants whose blossoms the birds feed upon, they will amply repay those gardeners who wish to attract birds. Car-

Annuals birds like

dinals, goldfinches, sparrows, chickadees, nuthatches, titmice, and towhees appreciate: abelia, aster, blessed thistle, buddleia, California poppy, centaurus, cosmos, forget-me-not, love-lies-bleeding, marigold, portulaca, prince's-feather, prince's-plume, rock purslane, sacaline, sunflower, tarweed or gumroot, zinnia.

We must not overlook that most surprising of all birds, the hummingbird. He may be attracted by a number of annuals or perennials, including: chinaberry or bead tree, columbine, coral bells, evening primrose, honeysuckle, jewelweed, morning glory, nasturtium, phlox, rhododendron, bee balm.

Here are some appealing plants and the sections of the North American continent where they can be grown. But remember that within each region there exist microclimates that must be reckoned with. For example, holly thrives in southern Massachusetts but is not hardy enough to survive the winter on the northern border of the state. And consider British Columbia, with its extremes ranging from lush rain forest to Arctic–Alpine conditions. Check with your bird-watching friends, your nurseryman, your county, state or provincial agricultural experts before you put shovel to ground!

Arrowwood Northeast, Middle West, Rocky Mountains, Great Plains.

Bayberry Northeast, Middle West, Southwest, Rocky Mountains, Great Plains.

Birch Northeast.

Blackhaw Northeast, Middle West, Southeast, Southwest, Rocky Mountains, Great Plains.

Blackberry Southeast, West Coast.

Cherry Northeast, Middle West.

Crab apple Northeast, Middle West, West Coast.

Greenbriar   Southeast, Southwest, Rocky Mountains, Great Plains.

Ground juniper   Northeast, Middle West.

Hawthorn   Northeast, Middle West, Rocky Mountains, Great Plains.

Hemlock   Northeast, West Coast.

Holly   Southeast, Southwest.

Honeysuckle   Northeast, Middle West, Southeast, Southwest, Rocky Mountains, Great Plains.

Inkberry   Southeast.

Mountain ash   Northeast, Middle West, West Coast, Rocky Mountains, Great Plains.

Mulberry   Northeast, Middle West, Southeast, Southwest.

Nannyberry   Northeast, Middle West, Rocky Mountains, Great Plains.

Persimmon   Southeast, Southwest.

Raspberry   Northeast, Middle West, Southeast, West Coast.

Sassafras   Northeast, Middle West, Southeast, Southwest.

Snowberry   Northeast, Middle West, Southwest, West Coast, Rocky Mountains, Great Plains.

Sour gum   Northeast, Middle West, Southwest.

Sumac   Northeast, Middle West.

Spicebush   Southeast, Southwest.

Virginia creeper   Northeast, Middle West, Southeast, West Coast, Rocky Mountains, Great Plains.

Winterberry   Northeast, Middle West, Southeast.

By planting and encouraging wildlife, you are doing something at least to make up for the devastation created by our throw-away consumer society. Good planting! Good luck!

Birds Get Thirsty, Too

We take water for granted. Turn on a tap and out it comes, hot or cold; if it doesn't, yell for a plumber. Only those of us who have lived through a drought in a house fed by what the old-timers called a "never-failing spring" know how precious water is.

What water means to us was made very plain during our second Fourth of July in our old house. We celebrated with a houseful of guests and a complete breakdown of our ancient water system. Water wasn't taken for granted again, ever.

After the guests and then the plumbers had departed, Will, Katie, and I were sitting out in the garden on a hot Sunday. It hadn't rained for at least two weeks, the lawn was browning, and the flowers were just getting by. The bill from the plumbers was so horrific that we didn't want to use the hose. The town's water bill on top of everything would be too much!

We were congratulating ourselves on being able to wash dishes and flush toilets once more. "Country life can be beautiful," Will said, lifting a cool beaded glass to his lips. Just then his eye fell upon a bird. Could it be one of those warblers? It was perched on a branch overhead, its wings outstretched, bill opened as if panting. We could see its tiny sides heaving. "What on earth is wrong with it?" he said. "I've never seen a bird act like that before. Do you suppose it's thirsty?" It had never occurred to us that birds could suffer thirst.

At that Will heaved himself from his chair and ambled off towards the barn. The ashcan lid he returned with was placed bottom side up in front of the flower bed and filled with water. We human beings sat under the trees and awaited the reaction to our offering. The thirsty warbler returned and viewed the improvised bird bath, but went no closer. Next a robin cocked his head first one way and then another at the water but he, too, refused to drink from it. Ah ha! here came a song sparrow. This brave little fellow would surely be the first to use our bath. But he also flew away.

What could be the matter? Perhaps it might be that it didn't look like a proper bird bath? We made plans to buy one. Our birds were evidently in need of something to drink.

Where, How Deep, How Much

Rob Jarvis, when asked to recommend a bath with all the best features because our birds didn't like ashcan lids, inquired where we had put it. "Of course they didn't alight on it. It's not that it's a lid, it's because you put it too near your garden border. The wise bird knows that it could be the hiding place for predators. Just move it out in the open and see what happens."

Placement of water

On a hot day anyone who can do so should put a pan of water in an open space, and then sit back to watch the birds. Just relax in the shade with a cooling drink in hand and watch the bird version of Coney Island.

We had learned the first lesson, to make food available. But birds' equal need for water we had completely overlooked. I imagine many well-meaning bird-lovers do as we did.

What every would-be owner of a country place dreams of is a purling brook wandering across his property. A dream is what it remains, as a rule. But how many of those who do own brooks know that birds, too, desire to nest near streams?

The need that birds have for water both winter and summer is simply not stressed enough. While the insect-eater and the berry-eater may get some moisture from the high water content of caterpillars and berries, the seed-eaters may avoid your home unless they are assured a good supply of fresh water.

Some Easy Baths and Mudholes

As in all phases of welcoming birds, attention must be paid to the sort of bird you have or want to have. The site in which to provide water, is, as we learned, most important. It must be in an open sunny spot from which a bird can fly off the moment it sees a cat start to make a spring.

The depth of water must be considered too. We overlooked this until it was pointed out that a little bird with short legs fears a deep pool just as a young child fears the deep end of the swimming pool. So be sure that some part of your bath has shallow, sloping sides—unless all you want to invite are swallows who simply graze the water as they fly over it. Or unless the long-legged heron is your fancy. I remember my aunt's formal garden, the focal point of which was a pool with a lion's mouth that trickled water into the quiet depths. It was lovely and its faint splash was wonderful on hot days. I didn't think of it then, but now I'll bet that Aunt Ruth never had a bird drink or bathe there. The sides went straight down for three feet. Birds would have drowned. Looking back, I don't think she ever consciously saw a bird in her life anyway.

It doesn't really matter to birds what form or shape your bird bath takes. High or low, big or small; fanciful fountain or just a lowly ashcan lid. But one and all have to be in the open, preferably in a sunny spot, where the bird will feel safe. For the lowest baths, this is mandatory. The traditional bath on a column placed against a background of shrubbery looks very handsome and has the additional advantage of being high enough in the air to thwart a springing cat. That being so, such a bath doesn't necessarily have to be in the open, making an exception to the rule.

But all small pools or baths have the disadvantage of drying up or getting stale if the water isn't replenished regularly. If I know anything about human nature, "something that has to be done" soon gets to be a chore.

Ground-level pools are fine when they are large enough to hold about fifteen gallons of water. That sounds like an awful lot of water, but there's the great advantage of not having to fill it up constantly. And furthermore, a quick splash of the hose will top it off and refresh it without effort.

It is important to remember that just as you must be conscientious about continuing to feed winter birds once you've started, so must you not neglect to supply water in the summer if you've begun early in the season. The water must be fresh to keep down the possibilities of disease, for when so many birds have accepted your invitation such a threat is always present.

Lest a fifteen-gallon pool appear to be a monstrous undertaking, let me reassure you. The owner of a subdivision plot made her particular property into a *Digging a pool* miniature wildlife preserve. She put in a pool. She did press a nephew into wielding a shovel for an hour or so, but she herself did a lot of the shallow excavating. Then she simply lined the depression with plastic and put stones around the outside to hide the edge, and put earth on the stones. She knew that plastic is slippery, and after a few disastrous tries the little birds would avoid her pool. So she simply smeared waterproof glue on the plastic sides and sprinkled sand on the glue before it dried. One end was made purposely shallow—about half an inch deep—for goldfinches, chickadees, song sparrows, and the little birds she hoped to attract. On the other side, the wading area for larger birds was deeper, perhaps one to two inches. The crowning and most imaginative touch, one which I'm sure we would have overlooked, was to place a pile of stones in the middle where the small birds could perch and splash about in safety.

Concrete would be much more durable, of course, but she was able to supply water cheaply and quickly for the birds she wanted to attract. Concrete pools naturally must follow her same general dimensions (not those of my Aunt Ruth's unwelcoming pool).

If something like this sounds too formidable a project, here's an idea for watering as simple as it can possibly be. Punch a very small hole through the bottom of a pail through which you push a length of string, then fill the pail with water. Hang the pail up in an open spot with a shallow dish under it. The string will let the water drip slowly into the dish and birds will have fresh water with a minimum of effort on your part.

Another refinement is supplying a trickle of water, just a very little that will produce a discreet muddy place. Swallows and robins, whose nest engineering demands soft pellets of mud, would be most grateful. If a trickle seems impractical, tending perhaps to turn into a flood, at nesting time a splash of the hose on a bare place, or a pailful of water thrown down, will do as well.

Why do birds seem to flock to spots that provide water? Perhaps, like us, they enjoy the freshness that goes with water. Most probably, though, the water attracts flying insects and aquatic bugs that, in turn, attract birds. Merely turning on a hose in a fine spray in the middle of the lawn will not have just children running through it in delight, but will also lure flycatchers and swallows in pursuit of bugs. Then a solemn robin may march over the damp ground looking intently for an unwary earthworm drawn upwards by the wet surface.

Attractions of water

Speaking of damp earth, the bird-conscious owner of property should realize that in drought years the worms on which robins feed simply burrow more deeply into the earth in search of moisture. The poor robin is unable to crack the tile-like surface for worms that aren't there. A soaking at night will tide over many a bird; this is true not only for robins, but also for any species that exists on grubs, worms, and caterpillars. In those same dry years the pools and baths of our gardens could be the only supply of water available to nesting birds and their offspring.

Why Birds Bathe

When the pool or bath or pail is finally in place, everyone's enjoyment begins. Take time to watch the birds splashing and drinking. Notice how they go about bathing. A bird doesn't plunk itself into the pool as we do into our bath. First, it dips the ends of its wings in the water. Then, touching the oily preening gland near the tail with its bill, it cleans each feather by drawing it through its bill, paying particular attention to the important flight feathers. Thus a water supply is vitally necessary not only for drinking but for keeping their most essential attribute, flight, in working order.

Not all birds are so temperate. Ernest Thompson Seton tells of an overheated robin who so enjoyed its bath that it stood all morning in the middle of a pool fighting off others, splashing and ducking. When at long last it had finally had enough bathing it was so waterlogged and its feathers were so soggy that it could hardly stagger away. But this bird seems to have been the exception. Most birds are more restrained. In hot weather chickadees are often content merely to stand in a pan of water just cooling their feet.

One other reason to provide water in the summer is to protect your strawberries and raspberries. Fruit-eaters will not be so anxious to devour them if another source of liquid is readily available.

Dealing with Winter and Freezes

Keeping water open

It's easy to understand the need for water in the summer, but not many people realize that birds need it in the winter as well. During a long cold spell of freezing weather without snow cover, winter birds get just as desperate as dwellers in the suburbs or the country do. This is the time when one's ingenuity is put to the test. Some experts have suggested that a straw-filled sack placed over a corner of a pool on a board will help to keep ice from forming. In a more sophisticated manner, one can use heavy-duty electric wire to install a submersible heater. But be careful! Water and electricity are bad companions. Our Rob Jarvis hangs a light bulb on a long cord closely over his water for birds. But he's careful to turn it on only when it is needed.

Other imaginative, if reckless, people have suggested using antifreeze or even a dollop of bourbon in a pool to keep it from freezing. Don't! Birds' systems are extremely delicate, and certainly can't cope with additives in their water supplies. The same goes for glycerine. It hopelessly mats feathers, and the bird would not be able to fly, and thus would be in danger of dying. Often we can best deal with the problem by getting out into the garden and breaking up the ice ourselves.

Whatever way it is done, see that water is available in a prolonged freeze when there is no naturally running water supply near by. If there is fresh snow on dried-up fruits or seeds, some moisture may be taken in, but as a rule a good water supply is as important in winter in attracting birds as it is in the summer. When you come down to it, water is probably the most essential factor to the survival of birds—more essential even than food.

We twentieth-century bird-lovers have to consider the acres, actually the square miles, of marshes, brooks, streams, and life-giving swamps that have been filled in or polluted. It behooves every concerned person to compensate for these devastating actions by any means possible, even doing so little as providing some fresh water in our gardens for the birds. Artificial sources of water are essential if we are going to have birds about us.

And There's the Dust Bath

"Bathing" doesn't necessarily mean "water" to birds. Ernest Thompson Seton said that birds take three kinds of baths: sun, water, and dust. Sometime, watch a bird take a dust bath in a patch of fine loose dirt. It crouches down, seems to loosen every feather, then by wriggling and scraping up dust with its wings, manages to cover itself thoroughly with puffs of earth. Straightening up, it quivers, then flies off, undoubtedly feeling as we do with a good dusting of talcum powder after a bath. But in the case of birds a dust bath has the practical purpose of helping to rid themselves of skin parasites.

We can provide dust baths quite easily by scratching and loosening with a rake a small area in a sunny spot and well away from shrubs. The resulting bit of raw earth is just what the dust-bathers are looking for. If that isn't practical or if the homeowners don't fancy scratching up a hard-won lawn, a tray filled with loose dirt will do as well. But again, be sure it's where birds have ample chance to watch for predators. In winter, after a fall of fresh light snow, you may see a bird take a snow bath in the same fashion.

While it's not likely that a town or village dweller will ever have an eagle or a buzzard take a dust bath on his lawn, it's interesting to know that owls, grouse, quail, and hawks like dust baths. They may well share your property with you, even if you are not aware of it.

American kestrel

Songbirds
and

Their
Enemies

The place of birds in man's scheme of the universe has been a matter of envy, greed, and cruel exploitation. The swans of mythology, Rome's eagles, the nobleman's falcons—all were expressions of the human wish to attract birdlike attributes to oneself. Saint Francis of Assisi embodied the vision of brotherhood among all living things. The twelve-and-twenty blackbirds baked in a pie, and the hundred million passenger pigeons shot from the sky were acts of those who saw man in control of all the beasts of the field and birds of the air.

The eighteenth century was noted for a sense of order, of balance. This sense impelled men to inquire into the machinery that made the orderly universe work. It was the beginning of scientific inquiry.

Early naturalists Amateurs such as Gilbert White, curate of Selborne, scrutinized in detail his English village and the farmland about him. The churchyard yews, the village idiot, the birds in the elm all shared Gilbert White's world, and all were considered by him to be equally of interest. They were as much a part of nature as he himself. His *Natural History and Antiquities of Selborne* has influenced generations of naturalists.

While the Gilbert Whites and others of the educated class in Europe were turning their attention to the natural phenomena around them, across the Atlantic the colonists struggled to survive in a strange environment. The land was there for the taking, if it could be subdued. In the subduing, animals, birds, people of alien cultures were destroyed or swept aside. The Indians who had killed only from necessity saw their birthright ravaged by the white man who imagined that the bounty would last forever.

A few tried to record the innumerable variety of birds, plants, and animals of the fresh and as yet unlimited land. John James Audubon, Alexander Wilson, and John Bartram and his son William are some of the benefactors who spent lonely years in the wilderness so that the new inhabitants could know and appreciate the wonderful creatures who shared the continent with them.

Then came the flowering of the Industrial Age, and its attendant labor-saving devices brought a degree of that leisure which for the first time allowed ordinary men and women to look up from their tasks and see what was going on around them.

As a result of this new interest, thoughtful people became aware that the bounty could not last: indeed, it was fast disappearing. The 1880's saw groups organized in an attempt to halt the hunting of songbirds for market. Later, people were appalled by the slaughter of the egrets, killed indiscriminately for their plumes to decorate the hats of fashionable women. The National Audubon Society, whose mission is to see the preservation of all natural resources, is the outgrowth of those concerned groups. The songbirds and egrets were finally allowed to live after years of struggle on the part of the Audubon Society and only after two Audubon wardens had been murdered by the plume-hunters.

One of the less fortunate results of this new-found interest in birds was that a number of those who became dedicated bird-watchers grew fiercely anthropomorphic and protective of what they considered to be their feathered friends. The bird books of the period are filled with passages such as ". . . my tiny companion, Mr. Chickadee, warmly dressed for the cold weather with his black cap pulled jauntily over his eyes and his scarf snug around his neck." The well-meaning writers and those who read their books tended to forget that the chickadee wasn't a tiny fellow human being but a creature who had evolved through millions of years to exist in a manner quite different from theirs. Assuming the role of protector, they recommended that their friends' natural predators be ruthlessly exterminated. A pioneer bird enthusiast who was instrumental in organizing bird clubs around the country, Ernest Baynes of Meriden, New Hampshire, told in his *Wild Bird Guest* how he shot hawks in his garden whenever he could!

Anthropomorphism

Man has a convenient way of dealing with creatures that he feels are interfering with him: give them a bad name. The very word "hawk" has acquired sinister connotations, and "hawklike" has been used by writers to depict characters having fiercely evil intentions. Victorians wept over deliciously morbid pictures of fat babies being carried off by eagles. Who knows what lambs or chickens that soaring bird had its eye on?

Predator persecution   It has taken a long time for farmers or sportsmen to correlate the destruction of hawks or other raptors with the increased depredations of rats and mice. It has been a slow process to teach lovers of songbirds that hawks aren't going to destroy their beloved flocks. The lessons have not been entirely learned even yet.

Some gamekeepers in Scotland learned the hard way. One year a number of them decided to shoot all the owls and hawks they could find in order to "protect" the grouse chicks. The following year, disease swept through the flocks and killed the grouse off anyway. The lesson to be learned was that raptors prey on the enfeebled and sick birds, thus preventing spread of epidemics.

The hawks that the fearful farmers and gardeners see are the large soaring birds whose numbers include the eagles. If they only knew that these birds are their friends! They seldom spot little, fast-moving hawks, darting among the trees, the so-called "bird hawks," who sometimes do prey on other birds.

Learning to Know the Hawks

Right here, before I go any further, let me give a word or two of encouragement about hawks and their identification. I almost gave up trying to bring order into my mind when it came to them. Bird friends would call out, "There he is, it's a sharp-shinned!" before I could even get my glasses focused on the fast-disappearing speck. "Look it up," they'd say; which was no help, for I was then confronted with "dark phase," "light phase," "immature and mature." When even the guidebook admitted that there was variation among individuals of the same species that could lead to confusion, I was in no mood to disentangle Buteos from Accipiters, names that my friends threw about so carelessly. A trip to a hawk-spotting sanctuary was no help either. All I got was a headache from black dots in the sky, lots of diagrams and lists. I was about to conclude that hawks were going to be a closed book in my bird life when someone said in the nick of time, "Just look for something that doesn't change: manner of flight, size, wing and tail shapes, bars, and body patches." Two days later I identified a red-tailed hawk all on my own. That did it. With new self-confidence I sat down and unraveled all the clues that help to make hawk watching fun and not frustrating. I made a list. Here it is.

All diurnal flesh-eaters, with strong hooked bills—commonly lumped together as hawks, but including vultures, kites, falcons, and eagles—belong in the order Falconiformes. "Diurnal" means daytime; which lets out owls, for they hunt mostly at night.

Falconiformes are divided into four families: I, Vultures; II, Kites, hawks, and eagles; III, Falcons; IV, Ospreys. That's the first step. Now to consider each family in North America separately.

Vultures (Cathartidae) have three subfamilies: 1) turkey vulture; 2) black vulture; 3) California condor. Vultures are huge black soaring birds whose wings are held in a shallow V and whose heads are so small as to make them appear headless. In contrast, eagles' heads can be seen.

Vulture

Kites, hawks, and *eagles* (Accipitridae) are divided into four subfamilies:

1) Kites: *a*, white-tailed kite; *b*, Mississippi kite; *c*, swallow-tailed kite; *d*, Everglade kite. Kites are now

Kite

Accipiter

Buteo

Eagle

Harrier

Falcon

rare in the United States and are found in only a few places in the West and South.

2) Accipiters: *a*, goshawk; *b*, sharp-shinned hawk; *c*, Cooper's hawk. These are the true hawks, rather small, with rounded wings, and long narrow tails that enable them to make sharp turns and swooping attacks below tree level. They are the "bird hawks" that will sometimes prey on songbirds and are hard to see because they don't soar.

3) Buteos and eagles: *a*, rough-legged; *b*, ferruginous; *c*, red-tailed; *d*, red-shouldered; *e*, Swainson's; *f*, broad-winged; *g*, Harris's. (There are five more Buteos that reside in the United States but they are very rare.) The task of Buteo identification is made somewhat easier because the range of Swainson's and ferruginous hawks is in the western half of North America, while that of the red-shouldered and broad-winged is in the Eastern half, and Harris's hawk resides only in the Southwest. Buteos are medium size to very large, with broad wings and tails that enable them to sail in a long soaring flight, seeking food on the ground. They are the "mouse hawks" that unfortunately present a large target for the unknowledgeable sportsman or farmer who doesn't realize that the Buteo is his best rodent-eating friend. Eagles are large Buteos, and there are two, the Golden and the Bald Eagle.

4) Harrier: There is only one in North America, the Marsh hawk or, as Roger Tory Peterson would have us call it, simply "harrier". It has a white rump.

Falcons (Falconidae): 1) gyrfalcon; 2) prairie falcon; 3) peregrine; 4) merlin; 5) kestrel; 6) aplomado. Falcons' long pointed wings, capable of tremendous speed, enable them to capture their prey high in the air. Their flight is choppy and rapid. They were the birds used for hawking in the Middle Ages. The gyrfalcon is an Arctic bird, and the prairie falcon lives in the West.

Osprey

Ospreys (Pandionidae) have a family all to themselves because, although they otherwise resemble their cousins the falcons, ospreys have two opposing toes on each foot and the pads have spines that help to clutch the fish the bird lives on. They have long crooked wings and are found always near water.

Luckily for all who love nature in its multitudinous parts, ornithologists such as E. H. Forbush in his monumental *Birds of Massachusetts* began to warn farmers back in the early years of the century that the success of their crops was directly influenced by the number of pest-eating birds about. Hawks and owls were eating their weight in gold in the numbers of rats and mice consumed; birds of every type were keeping insects in control. Man, for the first time, was beginning to suspect that he needed help; that with all his technological skill he still depended on the assistance of other creatures if he were to survive. So, gradually, the hawk-shooters began to realize that they were doing no service to anyone.

The hawk's duty in the chain of living is that of keeping the bird flocks in a healthy state by preying on feeble or diseased individuals. The number of birds must also be kept in proportion to the amount of food available for them. What trigger-happy Mr. Baynes overlooked when he "shot hawks whenever he could" was that the hawk was no more cruel to his songbirds than the songbirds were to the juicy insects caught on the wing. And it must always be remembered that the hawks have evolved along with the songbirds, and the songbirds have yet to be wiped out by the hawk.

In many states hawks and their relatives are not protected, although a great deal more still needs to be done to ensure that these magnificent creatures do not share the fate of the passenger pigeon. Even the continued existence of our national symbol, the bald eagle, remains in doubt.

Old Names for the Falcons

In order to speed up the process of education, Roger Tory Peterson has urged that the old English names, the correct names, be used for falcons. As he explains it, the only birds that are truly hawks are the Accipiters, those day-hunting "bird hawks," the Cooper's, sharp-shinned, and goshawks. But when the first settlers arrived, being men of generally little education they applied the word "hawk" erroneously to all birds of prey other than owls. The inherited stigma of the name has handicapped conservationists who are trying to educate the populace in the beneficent qualities of the birds. The words "duck hawk" or "pigeon hawk" brought to mind at once the image of the farmer's prize Pekin duck being carried aloft by a rapacious bird. To counteract this, Peterson has asked that henceforth the falcons be called by their correct names: "harrier" in place of "marsh hawk"; "peregrine" instead of "duck hawk"; "merlin" for "pigeon hawk," and "kestrel" in place of "sparrow hawk." These ancient names seem to have a ringing sound.

Whatever you call them, however, learn to identify their shapes as they perch or fly above you. Admire them for their skill at diving, their fantastic eyesight, and the speed at which they make their kill. The Accipiters may eat one of the songbirds that you consider yours, but generally the presence of any hawk is well warned by the jays and crows. For every kill the raptor makes, there are many unsuccessful tries. If Darwin is correct, only the unwary are eliminated.

Those nocturnal birds of prey, the owls, will rarely be seen. Their noiseless, night-time flight in the woods and fields keeps them from view of dark-fearing human beings. But if you do live where there are patches of woods, you may be lucky to hear on some late frosty night in early spring the sepulchral *who, who-who-ooo* as a great horned owl advertises for a wife. *Owls*

More Creatures with Bad Reputations

I must admit that although I have learned to be objective about songbirds and raptors, I do not like the "butcher bird." Katie and I happened to see the sagging body of a chickadee in a hawthorn tree. We thought at first that it had simply died, and had somehow got caught there. When we came closer we could see that it had been impaled on one of the tree's long, sharp thorns. Then I remembered the shrike and knew that this was his work; "shrike" and "shriek" had made a connection in my mind. Katie was upset. "Mom, I thought that the hawthorn tree would help birds, not be used as a bird butchershop." Lamely, I tried to give Katie an explanation of every creature's place in the universe, but I, too, held an unreasonable dislike for the bloody shrike. A few days later Will spotted him, a broad-headed bird, mask about his eyes, a strong bill curved downwards. We let him alone. He, too, had to eat; and he *is* a songbird. Perhaps what we dislike in him is that habit of impaling his victims, which reminds us too much of some of our own less pleasant qualities. *The shrike*

Jays and crows appear to be omnivorous, eating acorns, snails, grubs. Sometimes they eat an egg or two or a nestling, but certainly they are no threat to the survival of any species. Rather, they should be ap-preciated as the watchmen of the garden. During the winter we can induce a jay to leave the smaller birds alone at the feeder by providing him with some cracked corn in another spot.

Cats, dogs, mice, rats, weasels, snakes, squirrels, hawks—all are classified as enemies because they de-stroy or consume the birds or the plant material that we want for ourselves. But all have evolved along with man and songbirds. Cats are at the top of many birdlovers' hate lists. Of course, cats can't help their stalking and killing instinct. We who have invited birds to our garden have to live with cats who do their bit to keep down those other enemies of birds, the

Cat protection

mice and the rats. What one can do to foil cats is to put a shield around a particularly favored bird tree. A strip of pliable metal about a foot wide is wrapped around the trunk four feet up from the ground so that the cat's claws can't get any purchase. Put bird feeders on a metal pole or hang them from a branch. If it's your cat, feed it. Agnes we fed mightily. She bulged all summer and had to wear a humiliating cat bell. The vet told us that it wasn't the bell's warning the birds but rather that cats feel it is useless to spring (the vet, who was a kindly man, didn't know Agnes well enough to know that she had no intention of springing on anything). But we were now interested birders and felt that if we had the nerve to ask our neighbor to bell his cat, Agnes could not be favored.

We asked him also to keep his cat in at night during the nesting season because it's in the early morning that birds are active and feeding. We also asked his permission to scare her. The neighborhood was treated to the sight of Will bursting from the house at

Tree with cat shield

odd times, waving his arms and yelling. Whatever the

cats thought of it, it seemed to leave the birds free of cats during the dangerous time of nest-leaving.

Dogs can be another problem. Noisy ones may keep birds from becoming tame (but then so will a gang of children). Sometimes bird dogs with a keen nose may smell out nesting ground birds like quail or pheasant. So if you have dogs about, you might be advised to keep them restrained during nesting season.

Snakes, too, are predators. But they should not be destroyed, because they help keep insects and rodents under control.

A friend of ours had a pair of robins nesting in a low-growing vine near the door. One morning, to his wife's distress, a snake was squirming his way up to the nest while the parents tried in vain to drive him off. The friend refused to remove the snake, saying that it was nature's way of weeding out incompetent robins. Perhaps he didn't care to face the snake. There was a lot of hard feeling in the house that day.

Rats and mice are good climbers, but because there is so much food on the ground they seldom bother birds. Raccoons are destructive to nesting waterfowl. If you are fortunate enough to have a lake or pond bordering your place and you suspect Mr. Coon is enjoying the prospect of a duck-egg dinner, you may have to borrow or buy a Hav-a-Heart trap. If you are cleverer than he you can transport him to another part of the country without harming him. However, the best plan is to make sure that wildfowl have good cover.

Squirrels eat fruit and nuts—and rob nests. During early spring, when food is still scarce and birds are nesting, put out food for the hungry squirrel. Peanuts, sunflower seeds and, when you're making the umpteenth peanut-butter-and-jelly sandwich for the children, make some for the squirrels, who love them. Just put the squirrel food away from where you feed the songbirds.

The most destructive element against which birds have to contend, is—you guessed it—man himself. Shopping centers, urban sprawl, air and water pollution, introduction of pesticides, destruction of native habitat have taken an enormous toll of birds. We have wiped out the passenger pigeon, have almost eliminated the whooping cranes, and apparently the ivory-billed woodpecker and the condor are barely hanging on. The ospreys and peregrines and eagles are rarities.

Birds are adaptable, but wholesale elimination of their food, pesticides that poison them, and paving over their nesting sites—none of these can be overcome.

English sparrow

Birds and Man
Try to Live Together

One fine spring day ten or fifteen years ago, Will was out walking along our old stone wall where it rambles beside the town road. Years of neglect had allowed an untidy sprawl of chokecherry and what-have-you to edge out towards the pavement. In the past, the town sporadically contended with the scrubby growth by scything or mowing. This day Will saw the town truck moving slowly along, spraying a fine mist over the offending bushes. Will waved it down. Rachel

Carson's *Silent Spring* had just come out, and he asked, "Is this stuff safe?"

Two men leaned from the truck and smiled at him. "Gosh, yes. All the towns are using it. And man! What it saves on your tax dollar! Just two men instead of a whole crew. This spray sure keeps it dead, too. But it's safe, says so on the can. Why, I'll bet you could drink a whole can and it wouldn't even make you sick to your stomach." Will began to say, "Not right away maybe . . ." but they were already moving down the road, spray dripping from the chokecherry leaves behind them.

Herbicides   We never knew whether or not the driver did drink the can of herbicide, but we did know that sometime afterward there were reports of dead birds lying by the roadside or on lawns. Ordinarily it's really very hard to find dead birds unless they've been killed on your front doorsteps by a cat. Birds are so small that their bodies disappear easily into the grasses and undergrowth and disintegrate quickly. But the death rate among the songbirds in our area was so large that their bodies could not escape notice. The bird-lovers sounded notes of alarm but the town managers and selectmen stoutly insisted that the spraying saved tax dollars, and anyway what did a few dead little birds amount to?

The battle was hotly contested for a number of years, the roadsides looked like scorched earth, and the birds continued to die. Finally public opinion was aroused to the extent that the spraying was stopped.

That particular skirmish was won but the fight goes on. How on earth did we ever get ourselves into such a state?

When clumsy Archeopteryx, in escaping from a dinosaur, fell into a swamp, it disappeared. In time the mud that suffocated it hardened into slate and when it was discovered, 150 million years had gone by. Epoch had succeeded epoch, whole species of plants and animals had evolved and vanished. Biologists estimate the life span of a species to be about 500,000 years, and in the years that man and his forebears have been around—perhaps 2 million years—there have been almost four complete overturns of evolution. We appear to have done pretty well so far, merely to have existed three times as long as other species. It must be because we have been able to adjust to change.

We have only fossils to tell us what sort of animals and birds lived alongside our remotest ancestors. But these grandfathers and grandmothers of just 30,000 years ago, those who shivered in the last Ice Age, knew the cranes and condors as well as the now vanished saber-toothed tigers and wooly mammoths. The pitiful remnants of the once great flocks of those wonderful birds are hold-overs from the prehistoric era. It's true that man's habit of shooting anything that presents itself as a large and tempting target hasn't helped the survival of the cranes and condors. But it is true, also, that longterm oscillations of climate, food, and habitat are inevitable, and true that these birds have not been able to adjust to the changes. And if the species life span is 500,000 years, they may be at the end of their biological life.

"Obsolete" birds

For millions of years natural changes took place, age succeeded age, animals and plants grew and disappeared. Then we climbed down out of our trees, stood up, and looked about us. For a long time we were just another species of Mammalia existing along with other animals.

The inevitable changes took place, and we evolved into *Homo sapiens*, became agriculturalists, and eventually industrialists. And as industrialists we began to accelerate the natural pace of change. Men with machines feel obliged to use them. Huge cranes put up cities, bulldozers drain swamps, cars roll along billions of miles of pavement. In America, the most industrialized of nations, machines have been put to work with devastating effect. The change in their habitat has been so rapid that birds, animals, and plants have been hard put to survive. Many of them have not.

Across the ocean in Europe the landscape modification has not been so traumatic. The ancient cities grew slowly through the ages. The people fitted themselves into them as a fiddler crab fits himself into a shell. The birds have had time to adjust to the gradually changing habitat. In England the growth of the suburbs has been offset by the Englishman's love of gardens and trees, and the number of birds has actually increased to a density of thirty birds per acre—a much higher count than is found in woodlands.

Masters of Adaptation

When the first white men tramped through the woods where the traffic on New York's 42nd Street now roars, they reported that the song sparrows, vireos, and warblers created such a clamor that ". . . men can scarcely go through them for the whistling, the noise, the chattering."

Those songsters have long gone, departed from Manhattan, but birds have their ways of adapting if given a chance. The New York City of today harbors rock doves, night hawks, robins, chimney swifts, house sparrows, and starlings. Their nests are made of the twigs and leaves from the parks, the paper, string, and bits of material left about. Seeds, insects, berries, and discarded foods sustain them.

Some birds have positively gained by man's appearance on the scene. Even if the song sparrow, vireos, and warblers are seen no more along the forests of 42nd Street, the chances are, if you happen to steal along there on a summer evening, that you may hear a sharp *pee-ik* overhead. Because you are a bird-lover and because you have keen ears that catch the unusual noncity sound, you'll look up and see a night hawk sweeping overhead. Night hawks, who aren't hawks at all but members of the whippoorwill family, formerly had to make do with finding a barren, sandy, or rocky place in which to lay their eggs. Along came industrial man to put up flat-topped buildings by the thousands, and a flat-topped building was just what night hawks had been wanting ever since the first of them took to the air. To the birds the tar and pebble roofing looks just like their natural nesting sites; and best of all, their former predators, foxes, can't work elevators. The night hawks are thriving.

City birds

Barn swallows had to nest on ledges until white farmers came to build their barns all over the land. Indian lodges and tipis were obviously not suitable for swallow nests, but the dusky interiors of the high-roofed barns were exactly suited for the swallows' habit of nesting in colonies. Their numbers have increased rapidly.

Bank swallows think our road-cuts are splendid; and chimney swifts, who formerly nested in hollow trees, discovered the benefits of our chimneys. Now, alas, we have begun to tile our chimneys and the swifts are having a hard time of it, since the smooth tile affords no little ledges where they can attach their nests of glue and twigs.

Turkey vultures, those huge V-shapes soaring in the skies—nature's garbage collectors, essential to the landscape's good health—were once found only in the

Extending ranges

South. Interstate highways following the valleys northward provide the thermal updrafts needed to lift the vultures from the ground, with the result that now they are to be seen far north of their former range. For the vultures' food, the highways furnish the corpses of unwary animals killed by the cars speeding across what was their territory.

The enormous interest in feeding birds has enticed the mockingbird and cardinal to range far from their southern haunts and to remain into the winter months in snowy New England.

That denizen of Africa, the cattle egret, once seen only in the South, also has now wandered north, possibly as a result of the warmer winters in the past two decades.

When hayfields flourished near urban centers to feed the cities' horses, the population of ground-nesting bobolinks right across the United States and Canada was at its height. After 1900 their numbers began to decline as the urban hayfields were abandoned when the auto replaced the horse.

Ornithologists have found that a regular succession of birds moves in waves into abandoned fields. First the grackles and killdeer will appropriate a neglected cornfield; then, as the weeds and grasses begin to flourish, meadowlarks and vesper sparrows succeed them. Towhees and field sparrows like the encroaching briars and bushes, which in turn grow into the low trees suitable for goldfinches, waxwings, and indigo buntings. Last, the broad-leafed mature trees bring oven birds, redstarts, and hairy woodpeckers.

As our agriculture has increased its yields by farming with agribusiness methods, so have the populations of birds increased when they can feed on huge one-crop fields. The red-winged blackbirds, grackles, and starlings have become nuisances, attracted as they are to virtually limitless amounts of available food.

Martins have prospered with the numbers of fanciful multistoried bird houses put up for them on long poles.

On the other hand, bluebirds, never very numerous, have been adversely affected by man's activities. Until the middle of the nineteenth century, the bluebird preferred to live in the cities—which were, of course, a lot smaller, less polluted, and still contained orchards and gardens. Then along came the English sparrow, imported in the 1850's, who liked the same holes the bluebird did. When the bluebirds departed for the South, the sparrow, not being a traveler, moved into the vacated holes to spend the winter; and, being cheeky little Cockneys, refused to leave in the spring. When the bluebird saw those beady eyes peering out through the entrance of what had been his own nest, there was nothing for him to do but move to the country and become a country bird. Luckily for the bluebirds, in those days there were lots of orchards and apple trees with holes in them. But the unfortunate birds, symbol of happiness, survived only to face other and more insidious dangers: pesticides. The use of DDT has ceased, but not before killing great numbers of the lovely blue thrushes in whose body fat the persistent substance was stored.

Today we are using other herbicides and pesticides whose long-range effect on the food chain we know little about. It may be that the still diminishing number of bluebirds is due to their use and to the DDT still present. The more immediate cause is probably that the old country orchards once found on every farm have been turned into real estate develop-

Bluebird nest box

ments, and the modern orchards have been planted with scientifically maintained young plants. The old woodlands with lots of holey trees are subject now to carefully planned management. What natural nesting holes are still available are competed for by the aggressive starlings and house wrens. The only hope for the bluebirds is that bird-lovers will put up suitable nesting boxes to entice them to stay.

The English sparrow   As for the English sparrow who invaded the bluebird's domain, their numbers increased by leaps and bounds because their favorite food was the grain in the horse droppings, and as the cities were where most of the horses were concentrated, they became city dwellers in place of the bluebirds. The coming of the automobile diminished their numbers somewhat but today their cheeping, hopping presence is a welcome bit of wildlife in the concrete jungles that are our cities, and as such is welcome.

Happily, many of the songbirds have adapted themselves to the ways of man and, as in England, may even increase as the new suburban owners beautify their properties with trees, shrubs, and watering places. House wrens, robins, cardinals, bluejays, orioles, phoebes, catbirds, chipping sparrows, kingbirds, ruby-throated hummingbirds, and mockingbirds are those that have learned to live in the suburbs along with human beings. Even the wood thrush is learning to tolerate man and his ways.

And More Victims of Progress

But think of the other birds that nested near the farmhouses or in the pastures and woods and small towns of only fifty years ago! The eleven species just mentioned above seem a paltry number in comparison.

Where are the whippoorwills whose calls used to scare children so delightfully on summer evenings? The vesper sparrow from his singing perch above the pastures is heard less frequently. Should we blame developments encroaching on what was once farm land?

In Europe the birds, animals, and humans seem to have come to some sort of balance with one another. The patterns of work and society have been established for so long that sudden changes in the landscape are unlikely. On that continent, no species of birds have been lost in historic times. Would that we could say the same thing for ourselves! If the biologists are correct, the rate of natural extinction should be two species per century. Using this statistic, one could estimate that in the three hundred years that the white settler has had charge of the North American continent, six species would have vanished through no fault of man. Yet since the 1840's alone, four have disappeared completely and ten are in such dire straits that their survival is extremely doubtful. The great auk, the passenger pigeon, the heath hen, the Carolina parakeet were wantonly slaughtered. The number of our national symbol, the bald eagle, drops year by year, another victim of man's machines, his developments, and his pollutions.

Extinct and threatened birds

The peregrine falcon, that swift and beautiful bird of prey, has all but vanished from his airy cliffs, stricken by DDT.

The Ivory-billed woodpecker has not been seen for years. The Eskimo curlew, California condor, whooping crane, brown pelican, Hawaiian goose, and Aleutian Canadian goose are hard pressed for survival.

Almost too late, attempts are now being made to save the remnants of some of these birds. Experiments are going forward to introduce Arctic peregrines to the haunts of the native peregrines. Masked quail of the Southwest, victims of overgrazing, are being hand-raised in the Wildlife Research Center in Maryland. The effort to save the whooping crane is well known.

Implications of extinction

While the continued existence of a bird may be of little consequence to many people, the implications of its disappearance have a direct bearing on our health and well-being. That the falcons and birds of prey are faring badly rings a note of alarm for those alert enough to hear it, because their diminishing numbers mean that our own food is being contaminated. Raptors are at the top of the food chain, as we are. What is affecting them affects us, although we may not be aware of it as quickly.

As Dr. Douglas Lancaster, director of the Cornell Laboratory of Ornithology, said, "Why are men working to restore to nature a bird that the world might get along without? Perhaps it's because subconsciously we fear that our own species may suffer a similar fate."

We all have to exist together on this small planet. We are animals among others and must subsist on the same fragile chain of life. What affects the bald eagle affects us.

American robin

What to Do
'Till the Doctor Comes

I always thought that Will was a man able to handle with composure most of the crises of life. Until one summer evening when I heard him calling, "Jane, Katie, somebody—come and help!" We tore around the side of the house expecting to see him lying on the ground with at least a broken leg. There he stood holding something in a cupped hand, his free hand pushing his hair into a spike as he looked wildly about, mouth agape. "Don't laugh, for heaven's sake. I've got some sort of baby bird here and its just done something. I guess it's a bird. It's got wings."

Will disclosed a greyish lump of flesh with a few

An injured catbird

wild sprouts of pinfeathers on its head, its mouth gaping wildly. Where on earth had it come from? It was at the height of the nesting season and all sorts of birds had accepted our invitation to stay with us. We peered about without much hope. It was getting dark.

"There's some sort of nest up there in the apple tree," I offered without much conviction in my voice.

"Well, I'm not going climbing about in any tree in the dark. I'm going to put it in somebody's nest and hope it's the right one. I found it near the lilac bush. Anyway, in you go. Maybe it's a catbird." He pushed it into the nest.

He was right. It was a catbird and it had fallen from that particular nest. If we had been more experienced birders, we would have seen or heard the agitated parents scolding and calling, and would have realized something was amiss in the catbird world. In the case of this nestling, Will's instinctive action was probably correct because so young and helpless a thing would have had little chance of survival. We were certainly right in trying to find its home rather than taking it into the house to bring it up under the assumption that it was "lost." Becoming foster parents to a nestling is an undertaking not to be lightly assumed.

In the event of finding a young bird, one should remember that in most cases it is within sight of the parents and it is not lost. We were fortunate in that we had inadvertently put the little catbird back where he belonged, but it is safe to assume that anything that small hasn't gotten very far away. So look above you. If the nest has fallen, try to put it back or tie it with twine or use a substitute box, but be sure it has drainage holes.

By the time the next bird crisis occurred we were better prepared, mentally and emotionally. I was the one who almost stepped on a little morsel at the edge of the garden. The thin buzzing from its yellow mouth attracted my attention and I quickly scooped up Agnes, who usually did my Saturday morning inspection with me, and tossed her inside the house.

An orphaned wax-wing

We knew there was no danger of the parents' rejecting their offspring if we handled it, for birds have no developed sense of smell. The greatest danger in handling any wild thing is the terror and stress that it suffers as a result; enough, sometimes, to die of the shock, particularly if it is already injured. Being picked up and handled by human beings is as terrible for them as being carried off by a crocodile would be for us. If it is old enough to fly, the best thing is to simply make sure that it is as safe as possible, i.e., not out in the middle of the driveway where any passing predator can find it. At that age, it probably isn't lost, it's just having a flying lesson and has gotten beyond the limits of its strength. It's more likely that the parents are within visual range and know where the little wanderer is. Walk away, but keep an eye on it. Nine times out of ten it will recover its strength and courage and flutter off again.

What to do the tenth time? Well, take a deep breath, pick it up, and prepare to be a bird foster parent.

The little thing at my feet was buzzing away mournfully. It looked as if it had hatched very recently and was quite unable to do anything for itself. Where had it come from? The dogwood was the nearest likely place, and sure enough when I looked up above me I saw the remains of a nest that we had seen a pair of waxwings working on. We never learned what had caused the disaster. It might have been a predator, four-footed or with wings, which had destroyed the nest and the other babies, for we found two more little scraps of eggy birds lying near by.

Cedar waxwings are one of the birds that start to incubate before the clutch is complete, which is why our little friend was more developed than his dead siblings. Or, as we heard from Rob Jarvis, it's not uncommon for today's strange chemicals, used injudiciously, to enter a bird's food chain and affect its instincts so severely that the poor creature fails to act appropriately. In this case the waxwings had not built their nest properly. They may have neglected to provide a solid foundation.

Anyway there I was, stooped over a little bit of bird that I couldn't just walk away from. The nest was destroyed; the cedar waxwings didn't seem to be anywhere around. They'd probably left in distress.

The first thing was to see if the tiny creature was injured. I gently picked it up, extended its wings, flexed its legs. Sometimes you can tell if the bird has a broken leg by its not being able to flex its toes. It seemed to be in one piece, for its skin wasn't broken.

Warmth and Shelter

The next thing was to supply warmth, because it felt cold in my hands. A hot-water bottle was filled with warm water and the birdling was propped up by it in a small box. Then we riffled through our books for advice, and scouted through the house for something to put him in. It was important to have this new nest approximately the same size as the old one. An altricial bird, born helpless and without the ability to stand on legs that are doubled up under its body, needs the cupped sides of the nest for support and to give him purchase when he stretches up his head for food. Katie suggested an old nest that she'd collected, but it was vetoed because old nests are likely to harbor mites and parasites. The only container that seemed the right size was a small raspberry box, so we lined it with waxed paper and padded it well with Kleenex until its inner dimensions were about what we thought a waxwing's would be. It seemed to fit him well, since he didn't sprawl or fall over; our books said either was dangerous. And when we found what a lot of waste material went through that tiny alimentary canal we were glad that the Kleenex box was handy. The mother bird is usually the one to carry off the fecal sac and dispose of it away from the nest. We had the job now, and it required pretty constant attention.

It is best not to use any clipped grass because it is too cold, and shredded cloth or paper is dangerous because it might get tightly coiled around the little bird. Never put the nest in the sun. If warmth other than the hot-water bottle is needed, drape more Kleenex over him so that he can snuggle under it.

We set the substitute nest in a larger box on top of the hot-water bottle. The bottle was not efficient, for somebody was always having to think about keeping it hot. Later we were lent a heating pad, which, turned to Low, was just the thing. Lacking a hot-water bottle, two glass canning jars filled with hot water and placed on either side of the improvised nest will do, but of course they also have to be watched. The reason for the nest inside another box was so that if he did fall out somehow, he would still be confined and warm.

Food for a Tiny Invalid

Now the mite was lodged and warm, and the next emergency was to find something for his stomach. Its vital forces were probably very low from cold, stress, and lack of food. Will had remembered that warm milk with sugar or honey was instantly nutritious. But how should we give it to him? Katie's baby spoons were far too large; even demitasse spoons looked huge compared to that little beak. "Katie, dash across the road, they've got a new baby and they're sure to have an extra medicine dropper."

The milk and honey were ready but the bird wasn't. It refused to open its mouth. We didn't dare force it, because the beak was so soft that we were afraid it might break. I tried. Katie and Will tried. It steadfastly refused to open. Was it going to die of a hunger strike after all we'd done? We and the bird were getting tired and very sticky. We called the vet, who solved the problem: Press gently on either side of the beak at its base and it will open automatically. *Feeding* Now the once-more-warmed mixture went down like a charm. We were extremely careful to follow the vet's warning *not* to squirt the liquid down its throat. We fed the bird very slowly and made sure that it swallowed each time. Forcing too much at one time will go into its lung and drown it. Later Rob Jarvis told us that giving liquids is not a good idea: simply too dangerous.

Obviously a bird can't grow up on milk and honey, biblical as it sounds. More substantial provender must be found. What would it prefer? Different birds have different likes, as we'd discovered. If, as we guessed, this was a cedar waxwing, it would be started out on insects, and would graduate to berries, ants, and beetles when adult. We certainly weren't going to spend our time gathering them, but what to substitute? Rob came to the rescue and the way he described the menu, in the manner of a master chef, was a bright spot in a rather sticky day. All birds will eat a chopped-up hard-boiled egg yolk mixture moistened with oil and supplemented with a fine-grained cereal like baby cereal. This is good substitute food for insect-eaters of any age. To prevent their becoming crop-bound, the fruit-eating birds could have minced apple, cooked peas, and cut-up raisins soaked in water in addition to the cereal and yolk. A young robin might relish a little kidney cut in small strips. Hawks and owls will eat raw red meat, whole chicken heads, and any unwary rodent that has been trapped, for raptors must have roughage.

Precocial birds—pheasants, ducks, geese, and such—will pick up their own food and need the female only to protect them. But if you're convinced that the parent has permanently disappeared, you might offer some chicken mash with chopped eggs mixed in it, together with a small pan of water.

We decided that as this was a cedar waxwing we would start with yolk, oil and baby cereal formula because he was so small he would not be old enough to eat any fruit. His parents probably would have offered only soft, mashed insects.

The feeding this time wasn't as sticky, but was almost as messy. The beak-opening procedure had to be resorted to after we tried to offer bits of food on our fingertips. That wasn't satisfactory, for most of it ended up on the betoweled lap of the person holding the bird. Then one of us thought of having the mixture stiff enough to stick to the end of a toothpick to simulate the parent's beak. This worked beautifully, and soon the little bird opened its beak without having it pressed. Very soon, we found that tapping the side of the nest caused it to open its mouth at once. The slight disturbance of the parents' alighting on the edge of the nest is the signal to the nestling that food is about to appear. The baby then opens its mouth, thus triggering the parent to push food into the open yellow maw. We had to hold our bird when he was very young, but soon he grew so fast that holding no longer was necessary, and he pushed his head up whenever he felt our movements.

After the first 15-minute revival feedings we fed him hourly. The parents, of course, would have come more often but with less food, so hourly feedings of larger amounts kept him satisfied.

We gave him raw hamburger as he grew older, on the theory that it would be like the ants and beetles normal to his diet.

Out of the Hospital

Although we had been terribly lucky as amateurs in keeping the cedar waxwing alive, we were perplexed at how we were going to get rid of him. He was getting bigger by the day; we could almost see the feathers turn from those comical pin affairs to real feathery feathers. He was making strenuous attempts to hurl himself over the edge of that now-too-small raspberry box. His wings looked almost long enough to be of use. Only his tail lacked something in true proportionate length. The thought of letting him go before he'd attained at least a little knowledge of the ways of the world was distasteful to us, because we'd gotten fond of the little bundle of feathers and didn't want to have him gobbled up by the first hungry predator who came along. He should have a chance to learn to fly, at least.

We decided on putting an old Christmas tree in one corner of the screened-in porch, and setting in another corner an old coat rack that seemed to have as many arms as a tree. The idea was that here he could practice flying until he got the hang of it. If we couldn't catch him again to feed him, we'd leave food for him and hope he'd get the idea. It worked. If we laughed uncontrollably at his attempts to fly, he never knew. At least twice a day we were able to catch him without too much fuss and see that he was properly fed. We were now afraid that he was getting used to us. That would be a mistake, for a wildling should remain wild.

At last we judged that we had done as much for him as we could, and we carried him in his old box, covered with Kleenex, to an apple tree and wedged the box securely into a notch. Off came the covering, then we walked quickly back to the shelter of the porch. His head popped up and we could see him staring about at the wide world. Then he scrambled up the edge of the box, hesitated for a moment, and, as we held our breath, he made a flapping, unsteady journey to another branch a few yards away. He was on his own. We returned and went into the house. Katie sniffed a little quietly, and I swallowed.

Return to the wild

We were never sure of how he made out. At least we never saw any telltale cedar waxwing feathers strewn about the lawn. Sometimes we imagined that we saw him perched near by—and perhaps we were right. We hope he survived to make the long journey south, and that he returned next spring to our place with his mate.

Some Emergency Treatments for Older Birds

If we were fortunate with our first attempt to save a bird, we failed miserably the next time. Our new patient, a scarlet tanager, was caught with countless others of his kind in a late spring ice storm. Will noticed on the way home that some bright scarlet birds were crouching along the icy road. He and other careful drivers swerved to avoid startling them into flight, not realizing that they were exhausted. But there was one at the edge of our driveway, and we brought it in and gave it the same emergency treatment the waxwing had had. It was looking more alert—or so we thought—when we left it for the night. In the morning it was lying on its back with its tiny black feet curled in the air. We asked Rob what else we could have done, and he told us the chances were minimal that a wild bird would survive icy cold, hunger, and the terror of being picked up. A bird or any wild thing that is in poor enough condition to be picked up is in deep trouble already. Later we learned that the tanagers' migratory flight northward had been interrupted by the unseasonal ice storm, and that none of their usual food was available. They died by the thousands.

Lost birdlings and exhausted scarlet tanagers are one thing, robins with broken legs are another.

The door knocker banged hard one peaceful rainy October evening when Will and I were sitting down to our reading. Katie came into the room, followed by a bedraggled youngster holding in both hands an even more bedraggled robin. "Mom said you knew about birds," the child told us. "I found this near the back door when I got home from school. It sort of fluttered its wings and tried to hop away, but it just fell over on its side. We brought it in and tried to feed it, but it got even wilder and thrashed all about. I think its leg is broken." The two children looked solemnly at us. Will and I looked at each other. I'm sure he was feeling as squeamish as I was at the prospect of setting a bird's leg. We decided to see what we could do first, before taking the bird to the vet. Will said later that he didn't want to appear to back down on the job without trying to do it ourselves.

We gently flexed the leg and were pretty sure it was broken. Feigning a composure that neither of us felt, we issued instructions with the calm of an accomplished team of surgeons. "Tommy, just keep on holding the bird quietly. Katie, fill up the hot-water bottle and bring it here." Will went to get masking tape, which he cut into thin strips. Masking tape is easier to remove from feathers than is surgical adhesive tape. I called the doctor, who said he was sure that we could do the setting ourselves, since the bone wasn't protruding. To keep the bird from struggling, we'd need an old stocking with a hole cut in the toe, through which the bird's head would protrude when we pulled the body of the stocking over the creature. Next, another hole, through which to work on the injured leg. The good leg must be measured from the body joint to just above the claws, but the measurement should be taken while the elbow joint was bent. "You'll see why when you get it on," the vet said.

Setting fractures

Then the splint should be applied to the outside of the leg, tape run up the length of the splint, on up under the wing, across the back and chest, and attached to the top of the splint. It sounded complicated, I protested. "Just do it and you'll find out it isn't," he said. "But be careful to handle the bird gently. Remember, it's got hollow bones and they're fragile."

The splint was measured and cut out of thin cardboard so that it looked like an "L." Katie and Tommy had found and cut up an old stocking, and there seemed nothing for it but to set the bird's leg. I sat with a towel on my lap while the bird was fitted into its restraining stocking. A Kleenex was put over

the bird's head, since wild things are quieter if they can't see what's going on. Katie and Tommy were told to be still. As gently as we could, our hearts thumping almost as hard as out patient's, we fitted the L-shaped splint to the outside of the leg, which we bent to conform to the splint. The tape was applied as instructed—up the length of the splint, up under the wing, across the back and chest, and the free end wrapped around the top of the splint. We also wrapped tape around the leg and the splint; loosely, to prevent swelling. The job was done with much less fumbling than I'd anticipated. Finally we put the bird in a box with a hot-water bottle, covered the box partially, and left the bird alone for an hour.

When we returned with a bit of hamburger and cut-up soaked raisins, we found that he was resting on his chest with his other leg curled up under it in the same position as the splinted one, the roosting position. The chopped meat and raisins were left where he could reach them by stretching out his neck. We went to bed feeling fairly competent, but remembering the scarlet tanager and trying not to be too hopeful.

The next morning the hamburger was gone, the raisins were gone, and he'd managed to shift himself into the opposite corner. We continued to give him moist food, and kept fresh water available.

The reason for the L-shaped splint was soon very apparent, for the robin could scramble about with his good leg and could rest comfortably with both legs drawn under himself. It was obvious that if we had set the bird's leg with a long splint, the leg would have stuck out awkwardly and made it impossible for the bird to roost on his chest.

In fact, he was so comfortable that when we saw him flap his wings I'm sure that he would have flown if the box had been larger.

A bird's bones mend quickly. The vet thought it would be safe to remove the splint after two weeks, but we made doubly sure and kept him another five days.

It was a Saturday morning and appropriately a golden one. Katie held the feathery creature in her cupped hands with Tommy beside her. "Be careful, Mr. Robin, on your long trip." The black beady eyes rolled about, looking at the sky, its proper element. Then she flung up her hands, and out swooped the bird in a long glide to an apple tree. He paused as if taking bearing and then he was off, bound for the South.

Somehow we'd pulled the job off. Most of the credit, of course, went to the doctor for his advice; but still, we'd actually set the bird's leg ourselves.

Applied Commonsense

It is necessary to have experience and knowledge, or to know where to get advice, but elemental good sense is equally important. For instance, we knew wing breaks would be totally beyond us. They're a lot more complicated and more disabling than legs if they're set improperly. Birds have to have wings that function! My first reaction would be to take the bird to a vet. But perhaps with a good guide to follow, we might attempt that too.

One of the hard decisions that all animal-lovers must make is to forgo further medical aid when only prolonged suffering would result. There is no hard and fast rule. Each case must be judged individually.

Birds beyond help

We have not learned the correct method of killing a bird by snapping its neck. The other solution, using ether, seems to us to be difficult both in getting the stuff and quickly putting the bird out of its misery. We think it is easier for all to take the creature to the veterinarian.

Remember that, biologically speaking, a bird has not been saved unless it can take care of itself in the wild, and reproduce. This means that the sooner a bird is let go the better its chances are of making it on its own. Don't let it become too dependent. Also, and most important, that "lost" bird is probably not lost. Wait and see what happens before you decide to pick it up!

And remember that it is illegal to keep in captivity songbirds, owls, and hawks, since almost any bird except the starling and house sparrow is protected. As soon as you feel that emergency needs have been met, call the nearest nature center or game warden for advice.

Ruffed grouse

Venturing into
Kingdoms and Classes

I remember a trip we took off the Atlantic coast one summer. We asked the captain what certain black-and-white birds were. "Seabirds," he said. We weren't interested in birds then, but his designation seemed too simple, even to us. We found out later that they were eider duck.

A friend in Tennessee loves to hunt partridge. We said we didn't think that we had them around us. "You most certainly do," snorted Rob Jarvis, "some call them ruffed grouse." Grouse, quail, bobwhite, and partridge are all quite different, but their names are used interchangeably in different parts of the country. The United States and Canada are so huge that it's no wonder that the junco is a snowbird in another part of the country, that some people call the purple finch a linnet, and that a veery is a tawny thrush to some folk while others call a towhee a chewink. It does make for confusion.

The American Ornithological Union (AOU) has now standardized names for the entire country. It would seem that once you've taken pains to know birds by sight and perhaps by song it would be only sensible to know them by their correct names!

Local names increase the confusion by seeming to place birds into families to which they do not belong. For example, we call a meadowlark a lark, but it is really a cousin of the oriole and blackbird. Our robin was named by the first settlers because his red breast reminded them of the little robin they knew in England. The American robin is not like the English cock robin at all: he's really a cousin of England's sweet-singing thrush, the English blackbird. While the local common names may be easy to remember, they often are poor indicators of the actual relationship among birds.

American robin
English robin

As we became interested in the birds about us, we saw the fantastic variety of shapes, colors, and habits. The eider is different in so many ways from the hummingbird, yet they are both birds: they fly and lay eggs in nests. The web of similarity is interwoven with the woof of differences, making a marvelous pattern that is discernible for those who look. The pattern is indeed worth looking at.

The key to understanding it is in understanding the system of classification of natural objects, which sounds a lot harder than it really is. Of course, when we started out we were too confused even to glance at the scientific names. We paid no attention to terms like "family" or "order." But with a little confidence came the realization that these many different birds must belong in separate groups. The sense of order and pattern and even rhythm in the world about became so compelling that we were led imperceptibly into the study of how we and they fitted together in the universe. "Study" is too formal a word for what we did: we looked, and, because the whole concept was so very interesting, we couldn't keep ourselves from thinking about it.

Taxonomy

Imagine the confusion of the early natural scientists of North America when they tried to make sense of the bewildering profusion of plants, fishes, animals, and minerals surrounding them. It took the ingenious men of the Enlightenment in the eighteenth century to bring order out of chaos. They did it by sorting everything into smaller and smaller groups so that at the end the little chickadee fits as neatly into its own niche as does the largest lunar boulder. It was almost as if they had a vision of the beauty of orderliness.

They went about it this way. First, all natural objects were divided into three kingdoms: vegetable, animal, and mineral. The animal kingdom embraces all us living creatures, from lobsters and mosquitoes to eagles and human beings. Next, those eighteenth-century geniuses divided the animal kingdom into "phyla," plural of the Latin "phylum," meaning tribe or group. To one phylum they gave the name "Chordata," meaning possessed of a spinal cord; and here the vertebrates—among them we humans and the birds—part company from the mosquitoes and lobsters, who belong in another phylum. The Chordata in turn were broken down into classes, with man going into one class, the Mammalia, and the birds into the Aves (from the Latin "avis").

Each class is then subdivided into orders. And this is where the fun of bird nomenclature begins, and where it all falls into place so neatly.

How could we possibly deal with the 8,544 different species—that is, particular kinds—of birds unless previously they were grouped into 27 orders? Without the orders we'd be tempted to lump cranes in with herons, but the zoologist, by considering the form of the birds, their internal structure including blood serum, bone construction, and muscles, determines that the cranes belong to the Gruiformes order, and the herons—along with their cousins the spoonbills, ibises, egrets, storks, and flamingos—to the order Ciconiiformes.

Bird orders

The 27 orders start with the most primitive, the Struthioniformes (ostriches), and end with the most evolved, the Passeriformes, which are birds capable of perching.

Within each order are the families, and from the number of families in each order it is possible to tell how the larger group is faring in our industrialized world. The most primitive order, Struthioniformes, has only one family, the ostriches; the Gruiformes, the cranes, have only three families; and the Falconiformes are less hard-pressed, with six. But how the Passeriformes have succeeded! They possess 55 families in the order, testimony to their very successful job of adaptation.

We started slowly, taking the easy way of learning the names of orders of the birds around our place. It was simple, because most of them were Passeriformes. The crows, jays, flycatchers, swallows, chickadees, titmice, nuthatches, and creepers, wrens, thrushes and bluebirds and orioles, finches and sparrows, vireos, kinglets, warblers, blackbirds, larks, mockingbirds, waxwings, shrikes, starlings, grosbeaks, and tanagers—all are Passeriformes! Most of the songbirds, in fact.

The woodpeckers are a separate order, Piciformes: an easy one, because it sounds like "picking" to us. The hummingbirds are easy, too, for they and the swifts are Apodiformes, so called because "apod" means footless, and these hovering birds appear to have no feet. Cuckoos, anis, and roadrunners are almost too easy, for their order is Cuculiformes. Vultures, hawks, and falcons are Falconiformes. Pigeons and doves are Columbiformes; owls are Strigiformes, and nighthawks and whippoorwills belong to the order Caprimulgiformes. Thus in eight orders almost all the land birds are collected. By learning the arrangement of orders you can save a lot of time in finding the group you're looking for without having to refer to the index of the guidebook.

The orders are broken down into families; the next-to-the-last step is to separate into subfamilies, called "genera" (plural of "genus"), consisting of one or more species. Finally, at the end of the road comes the specific bird, and here for the first time the word "specific" took on its full meaning for us, since it's derived from the word "species."

The system of naming the species has a logic all its own, thanks to that most ingenious of all great eighteenth-century scientists, Karl von Linné, a Swede most commonly known as Carolus Linnaeus. *Linnaeus* The first attempts to name specific birds resulted in long, impossibly clumsy appellations that actually defeated the purpose of making easier the identification of natural objects. Linnaeus invented the binomial system, in which each species first was given the generic name—the name of the genus, always capitalized on the first letter—followed by the specific name as the second part. The black-capped chickadee belongs in the family Paridae, which includes all chickadees, but he is given his own identity by combining part of his family name, "Parus," with his very own name "atricapillus," to make *Parus atricapillus*. The Carolina chickadee, his cousin, is *Parus carolinensis*. If you're speaking, or trying to, to a Hungarian bird-lover about chickadees and use these terms, he'll know precisely what you're talking about. Local names are local; scientific names are international. The beauty of the order and the pattern seemed to us to be almost cosmic.

Let's do the family tree of the mockingbird, whose formal name expresses so well his outstanding characteristic: Kingdom—animal; phylum—Chordata; class—Aves; order—Passeriformes; family—Mimidae (from the Greek root meaning "imitate"); genus—Mimus; species—polyglottos (meaning "many-tongued" or "speaking").

So the mockingbird is *Mimus polyglottos*, the many-tongued imitator.

Northern oriole

Strings and Boxes,
Seeds and Suet

John Terres tells of an old lady who shook out of her bedroom window every spring a fistful of feathers from her pillows. After their first surprise the birds seemed to expect her offering, and every year they would fly up and look expectantly through the window. What will happen when poly-this and poly-that take over from feathers? Will birds learn to adjust to polys?

We heard of a pair of orioles that plucked hair from the head of their benefactor. This appears to be going too far, but you might put out lengths of bright ribbon or string for them. Not too long, though, for the orioles might entangle themselves: six or eight inches will do. Hang yarn, thread, or string over a branch and see who takes it.

Nest materials   Horse hair is greatly prized by many perching birds. Persuade your horse-loving adolescent to save some mane and tail groomings for you. And hair of the short fluffy kind is a favorite for nest-lining.

If you think you have some flycatchers about, hang out some strips of cellophane for them. They insist on weaving discarded snake skins into their nests as protection against predators, but will use your substitute. We have a relative who each year brings up a hank of Spanish moss from the South and hangs it in her Cape Cod pine trees, a thoughtful gesture much appreciated by birds that are building nests.

There is also the true story of a greedy robin who was found to have incorporated a ten-dollar bill in her nest. You can encourage the less expensive tastes of robins, wood thrushes, and phoebes by having some mud available, perhaps in a shallow pan. They need mud for plaster.

Don't forget to leave some old bulrushes standing if you're so fortunate as to have them. The fuzz is used as lining by many birds.

We weren't patient enough or possessed of nimble fingers to take apart the red-eyed vireo's nest that we had found our first fall. At a nature center someone did and separated all the materials the vireo had carefully fastened together, and labeled and mounted them as an exhibit. The list was impressive: birch-bark bits, vine fibers, spider-egg case, plant down, bald-faced hornet's nest, bark fibers, bark/dirt, spruce twigs, wood chips, grapevine. It makes me tired just to think of collecting all that.

But the work of one European redstart must be the world's championship in collecting. Someone counted

361 stones, 15 nails, 146 pieces of bark, 14 bamboo splinters, 3 pieces of tin, 35 pieces of adhesive tape, 103 pieces of hard dirt, several rags and bones, 1 piece of glass, 4 pieces of inner tubes and last, but not least, 30 pieces of horse manure! One wonders where the eggs were fitted in.

A Helping Hand for Nature

We've been talking of helping the birds who nest in trees, but for those who nest near the ground—field and song sparrows, bobolinks, brown thrashers, veeries—a discreet brush pile will do very nicely. *Ground-nesters* During late winter, prunings from trees on your place can be piled in a remote corner. Or, lacking trees big enough to prune, you'll find it easy enough, heaven knows, to get as much brush as you need from overgrown roadsides. A cover of evergreens should be renewed every year, possibly with the old Christmas tree cut up and laid on top to provide a thatched roof. Every two years the whole affair should be carted off and a new one started, for as the pile sags with old age, it collapses, leaving no space for the birds who want to shelter in it in winter or to build nests in its twiggy interior in the summer.

We inadvertently provided what amounted to the Ritz of bird apartments. During a violent summer thunderstorm one of the ancient apple trees was struck by lightning. After the tempest had growled off to the east, we inspected the ruin. Gnarled branches lay entangled like the remains of an old elephant. Our first impulse was to cut it to the ground and dig out the roots. However, the more we studied the project, estimating the time and expense of doing it ourselves with the tools we had or hiring someone else to do it, the more we hesitated. Finally we decided to do the very easiest thing, which was to cut off the broken limbs and make the trunk look as respectable as possible. Then we got from a nursery a number of sturdy well-grown ivy plants and dug them into the soil around the old wreck. It took some time before it lost its skeletal look, but now it's a fountain of leathery green leaves the year round. And we have in our front yard the most perfect bird sanctuary possible. It's tall enough to discourage Agnes, a lazy cat anyway, and to entice birds to roost. But best of all is its trunk, around which thick ivy branches have intertwined to produce a dense canopy of leaves. In winter the chickadees and nuthatches get out of the rain and away from the wind. In summer the tenacious branches provide support for a number of different nests whose occupants are grateful for the green shady umbrella.

When we realized that our trees and shrubs simply did not provide enough variety and number of nesting sites, we knew that we had to furnish something for birds to nest in, for we and they couldn't wait for our planned plantings to grow to maturity. Bird *Bird boxes* houses—or, more correctly, bird boxes—would have to be available.

Learning that we were puzzling over how best to do this, a loving great aunt sent Katie for her birthday a do-it-yourself kit for making a bird box. The thing looked enormous in its carton, and it was still enormous when Will and I and Katie managed finally to assemble it. Faithfully following instructions, somehow we were able to hoist it up in the air—all four feet of it—and hang it from a stout limb, where we and the birds eyed it dubiously.

"Do you think the hole is really supposed to be at the bottom like that?" Katie wondered. "I'll bet it's like a chamber of horrors up inside, all dark with little nasty corners. I think it's awful and I'm glad Great Aunt Anna lives in California because, Mum and Dad, you're going to help me take it down right away."

Now it rests in a remote corner of the barn, unused—but now right-side-up, with entrance hole at top.

We knew there were plans available for making boxes but Will, no carpenter to begin with, didn't want to start on a project only to find that it had turned out to be another monstrosity.

Man-Made Houses (and a Checklist)

As we had learned with other problems, when in doubt go to someone who knows. In this case, the Vermont Institute of Natural Science. Their philosophy on houses was interesting: "Although we call man-made nesting boxes 'bird houses,' keep in mind that birds use nests or nesting boxes only as cradles for the eggs and nurseries for the young birds. Nests are not 'homes' for the birds, but are used for the specific purpose of protecting and warming the eggs and young."

We knew from watching that first catbird family that eggs must be kept at a constant temperature of 90 to 100 degrees Fahrenheit. A nest is of great help in conserving and holding in the necessary warmth. This is a matter particularly important when birds nest in early February, or when cold spring rains occur. Even a slight depression made by a killdeer in sand or gravel increases the eggs' chances of survival.

The Institute said that the construction and erection of nest boxes is a simple, rewarding project for individuals or groups of all ages. When Katie came home from school with a bluebird's box she had made, there was nothing for it but that Will had to try his hand too. Nobody was more surprised than he when a tree swallow inspected the newly made house, and in a day or two started to bring straw. He said it was worth his smashed thumb.

According to the Vermont Institute of Natural Science, bird boxes and similar artificial nests have been known to attract as many as fifty species of American birds. "Undesirables" like English sparrows and starlings covet bird houses, so if you wish to encourage the native species, it is necessary to discourage the attempts of these interlopers to take over the nesting boxes. You should remove these intruders' eggs and clean out nesting material as fast as it is collected. English sparrows and starlings have had a devastating effect on the bluebird population, and only by providing alternative sites can the bluebirds' continued existence be assured. But take care that the correct dimensions are followed, or the intruders will be able to squeeze in.

Evicting undesirable tenants

Small rectangular shelves put up in convenient places—such as under the eaves of a garage or shed—will attract robins and phoebes, who refuse to nest in an enclosed box. If you can't put the shelves under a ready-made overhang, put a little roof over them.

Here are some general recommendations for building or supplying nesting boxes:

When you're building an artificial nest, remember that birds have specific preferences, so building an "all-purpose" nest will be just a waste of your time.

Be careful not to make the entrance hole too large.

Drill some small holes in the floor of the box for drainage.

Tin cans as nests can be death traps, because of the heat from the sun. Wood is the best material.

A few small slits or holes through the walls below the roof overhang will give better ventilation.

Guard the nesting birds from climbing cats or other predators by placing the boxes on metal posts, or putting metal guards on the posts.

The entrance should not be towards the prevailing wind.

Clean out old nesting materials before birds return in the spring. To make this task easier, the box should be made so that it can be opened easily.

Martin houses are painted white to reflect the sun, but dull colors are better for the outside finish for all other birds.

Birds are more apt to use a house if it is stationary and not swinging from a limb.

Gourds make economical bird houses.

New boxes should be set up in the fall to allow them to weather over the winter and be more acceptable in the spring. Also, nuthatches, downy woodpeckers, chickadees, and other hole-nesting birds will have a sheltering place in which to roost on cold stormy winter nights.

Use ¾-to-1-inch wood—cypress, white pine, cedar, yellow poplar. To have the box last longer, use brass screws, brass hinges, and galvanized or brass nails. Steel nails will rust. Sharp changes in temperature will cause nails to loosen and pull out, so screws are better.

The United States Department of the Interior has for sale a bulletin titled *Homes for Birds*. Write to the Superintendent of Documents, U.S. Government Printing Office, Washington, D.C. 20402.

Following is a list of dimensions suitable for various species, recommended heights above ground for placing boxes, and some further general notes.

Tree swallow, Carolina wren, Bewick's wren, violet-green swallow   These prefer to have the height of their boxes (inside, roof to floor) to be 6 to 8 inches, and about 4 inches deep (front to back) and 4 inches wide. The diameter of the entrance is highly important, because birds are most pernickety about it! The Carolina, house, and Bewick's wren all require an entrance hole to be 1¼ inches in diameter. A tree swallow will accept one a trifle larger: 1½ inches in diameter. A tree swallow likes to be within two miles of a lake, a Carolina wren likes to be near thick underbrush, a Bewick's wren would prefer thick hedges near by. The three wrens look for boxes 6 to 10 feet above the ground, while the two swallows like theirs to be 10 to 15 feet in the air.

Nuthatch, chickadee, titmouse, bluebird   All require their boxes be 8 to 10 inches tall, 4 inches deep and 4 inches wide; however, the bluebird would like it to be 5 inches wide. The chickadee entrance should be 1⅛ inches in diameter; for nuthatches and titmice, 1¼ inches; for bluebirds 1½. The nuthatch is happiest with his house hung high—12 feet at least above ground. Titmice and chickadees like 6 to 15 feet in the air; the bluebird likes its box to face an open field and be 5 to 10 feet above the ground.

Song sparrow, house finch, purple martin   These prefer boxes 6 inches high inside, 6 inches deep, 6 inches wide; entrance hole 2 inches in diameter. Song sparrows and house finches both want their boxes to be 8 to 12 feet above the ground. The purple martin likes its box 15 to 20 feet up, and also wants to be in the open and have no tall trees near by.

Golden-fronted woodpecker, red-headed woodpecker   Both want boxes 12 to 15 inches tall, 6 inches deep, 6 inches wide; they want a 2-inch-diameter entrance, and to have the box 12 to 20 feet in the air. The red-headed woodpecker would like some sawdust near by for nest material.

Hairy woodpecker, flicker The general dimensions for the woodpeckers above suit the hairy to a T, but his entrance hole must be only 1½ inches. The flicker doesn't want quite so tall a box: 8 to 10 inches will do. The rest of the dimensions are suitable, but the boxes don't have to be quite so far above the ground—6 to 20 feet is acceptable. They also would like sawdust near by.

Downy woodpecker More modest in his requirements: 8 to 10 inches tall, 4 inches deep, 4 inches wide; entrance hole 1¼ inches. Any height over 6 feet in the air will suit.

Crested flycatcher Looks for a box that is 8 to 10 inches tall, 6 inches deep, 6 inches wide; entrance hole 2 inches in diameter. The whole affair should be covered with bark and located in a secluded spot.

Owls Screech owls can be attracted to a box 12 to 15 inches tall, 8 deep, 8 wide; entrance hole should be 3 inches in diameter; box placed 10 to 30 feet in the air, and at the edge of a woodlot. The saw-whet owl will be happy with a box 10 to 12 inches tall, 6 deep and 6 wide, with an entrance 2½ inches in diameter; box located 12 to 20 feet from the ground.

Feed for Your Birds

Some bird-lovers recommend feeding year round, an artificial procedure you might say, but man's intrusive actions have already upset the natural balance of wild things. Year-round feeding encourages the continued presence of birds who would otherwise leave for easier feeding, and attracts those who winter in your area and might lack for food.

If this seems to be too much work you might at least consider starting in mid-August when birds are making up their minds. But most important, regardless of *Feed consistently* when you begin: *don't interrupt the feeding!* If you fear that you won't be able to continue, don't begin. Failure could cause hardship for the birds, and might mean their death.

Birds who visit feeders may be divided into four groups:

1) Seed-eaters who gather their food from the ground. Native sparrows belong to this group. They eat the seeds and small grains that have dropped from feeders or have been scattered.

2) Birds that prefer to feed four or five feet above the ground—a group that includes evening grosbeaks. Their staple food, sunflower seed, is hung from a branch or a pole.

3) Insect-eating birds, such as woodpeckers and chickadees, like to have their food, suet, and peanut butter well above the ground. Chickadees also like sunflower seed.

4) The last group of birds may be lumped together because they are too individualistic to list separately according to food preferences: mockingbirds, wintering orioles, and an occasional meadowlark, or other seasonal exotic.

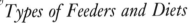

Types of Feeders and Diets

An ideal feeder to start with is a tray or platform, set up on a pole or hanging. A tray feeder should have a roof to protect the seeds, a raised edge to keep them from blowing away, and a hopper for easier feeding. A windowsill feeding tray can be a delight, particularly with a glass roof that allows you to observe your visitors. But warn your children not to make sudden movements that startle the birds, especially if a completely see-through lucite feeder is used.

Birds prefer to feed in the sun and out of the wind, and are particularly hungry for food early in the morning. Therefore the feeding place should have a southern exposure and as much shelter as possible.

Birds are less wary of your feeder if there is some shelter or cover near by. Shrubs, trees, or a home-made brush pile are fine.

Here are the most useful store-bought feeds:

Sunflower   Without a doubt sunflower seed is the most important food to supply for wild birds. A medium black-striped variety seems to be most practical, and of a quality consistent with good feeding and diet requirements. Look for a seed that is clean, fresh, and free from sweepings or waste. Purchases in 25 or 50 pounds are practical.

Thistle seed   Ideal for attracting most of the finches and sparrow families. This seed has an excellent food value, due to its high oil and protein content. It is growing in popularity among people who feed birds.

Cracked corn   Wild birds are attracted to cracked corn because of its high nutritional value. Popular with some bird-lovers because of its relatively low cost and its attraction for mourning doves and field birds.

Special mixed seed   This is an excellent quality seed, a mix based on reports and studies at several nature centers and Audubon organizations. It contains a minimum of one-third sunflowers, with two-thirds a mixture of peanut hearts, white millet, fine cracked corn, and thistle seeds. A superb mixed seed for people serious about feeding birds.

Bird seed

The best food to start with in a feeding program is a standard all-purpose item, a bag of mixed bird feed of the type that may be bought at a supermarket, hardware store, garden store, or from a conservation organization. Most commercial seed mixtures contain a maximum of inexpensive millet, other small seeds, and cracked corn, and a minimum of relatively expensive sunflower seed. When you first start feeding, watch and see which foods are the most popular. This is a very rich feed, and costly, but it attracts several bird species.

A complete feeding program should have suet. Beef kidney suet is best. Bacon fat or other cooking fats can be saved and used. Peanut butter is another standard item, but is much safer when mixed with stale cereal or grains, to prevent any danger of birds' choking on straight peanut butter.

Most native birds are quite specific in their food requirements. Some visit feeders in search of a single item. To attract a wide variety of birds, you must put out a wide variety of foods.

You will find that thistle seed attracts certain birds—especially the smaller northern finches and goldfinches are delighted with it!—and requires a special feeder; but it lasts for a reasonably long period of time.

Nuisances Around Feeders

"There's that darned squirrel again!" And Will bounds to his feet and raps sharply on the window. Outside on the feeder the squirrel flicks his tail and continues to munch expensive bird seed. No sooner is our breakfast resumed than in a swirl of blue the jays settle in for their morning meal. "Darned nuisances," growls Will.

But be warned lest you, too, be regarded as a nuisance by your neighbors. Indiscriminate and careless feeding will attract all sorts of pesky creatures to your property and that of your neighbors, who will not be happy with the sight of pigeons, house sparrows, and rats frisking about. Exercise moderation in the where and how of feeding.

You can also deal with house sparrows and starlings by throwing cracked corn on the ground at some place distant from where you have the feeders containing food that is more expensive. Squirrels can be foiled by hanging cylindrical feeders. However, the Vermont Institute of Natural Science says that one might as well become philosophical and recognize that feeding programs upset the balance of nature and attract unnatural gatherings of wild visitors.

Two final reminders:

Birds must see the food, otherwise they won't find it. Use uncovered feeders so that the food can be plainly seen until the birds know it's there.

Birds are creatures of habit, so if you begin to feed them in the fall, keep it up regularly right through the winter and into the spring. During a sudden change into bad weather, the birds might not survive until the next day if they can't find food.

Canada goose

Goodbye: We'll See You Next Year

Towards the end of July in the northern United States and the southern part of Canada, the lovely bird symphonies will gradually cease, the males singing only snatches of their songs. The parents have raised their broods and now they're tired and thin from the constant search for food. They must rest and gain weight for the winter or for the long trip south. The young birds are busy learning the tricks of survival and gathering strength for what lies ahead.

Not all birds migrate. Some have adapted to severe conditions and remain out of choice; others may not be in condition, and thus lack the urge to leave.

Once nesting is over, many species will revert to their gregarious nature and start to flock, a sort of sociable survival which provides more eyes to see food, more bills to snap up insects, and less danger from predators. Cowbirds, who have no nestlings to care for, will be among the first to flock, often as early as June. In midsummer the young of the first broods are left to fend for themselves, and they also congregate.

Fall migration

With the passing of the longest days the more delicate birds with the farthest to go will begin to leave. Flycatchers and swallows will start to flock in August; then the warblers, swifts, and night hawks. Hardy warblers will stay until October, for they can eat the berries and seeds that the more specialized warblers cannot. The phoebe, an insect-eater, will leave when his supply of insects runs out, but the robin, who gets worms and grubs from the soil, can stay later because he can switch to late berries.

Generally settled weather in the autumn and the presence of juveniles mean that the birds leave gradually, so the fall flitting lacks the spectacular wavelike crests of the spring migration. The shortened days with less light cause birds to undergo changes in their pituitary and thyroid glands; it is during these changes that the birds quietly leave. In the spring the increased light through the eye stimulates the glands and reproductive system, which in turn trigger the urge to migrate and mate.

In March as the food supply slowly becomes available, the red-winged blackbirds, robins, crows and flickers start north, flying about forty miles a day and taking as much as fifty to eighty days, finding plenty of insect food among the newly opened leaves. The vireo takes only a week to make his passage, and at the

Spring migration

end of May the hummingbird arrives as flowers bloom.

Smaller birds are night migrants who need darkness for protection. The wood warblers, thrushes, vireos, flycatchers, orioles, and some sparrows generally fly at an altitude of about 1,000 feet and at a speed of 25 miles per hour, spending some of the daylight hours feeding. The diurnal migrants are loons, terns, gulls, hummingbirds, swallows, swifts, hawks, and nighthawks.

The Mysteries of Migration

Why do some birds migrate and others stay behind? The rose-breasted grosbeak goes to Central and South America, but his cousin, the evening grosbeak, sticks it out in the winter from Missouri to New England. The Arctic tern flies from the ice that encircles the South Pole to spend the summer near the tip of Greenland, while the sooty tern chooses to stay close to the Dry Tortugas summer and winter. We don't know why some leave and others stay, but naturalists have theorized that originally all birds were tropical, and that at the end of the last ice age the very pressure of population forced many species to migrate to the new land to the north. That birds continue to migrate may be the result of evolutionary demands. Migration has prevented the extinction of those species who are unable to adapt to the conditions of any one region year round. The very act of migrating, though, carries with it a vastly increased chance of mortality.

How birds migrate remains a mystery. Think of the small birds who fly for 36 hours from South America directly over the Caribbean to the Gulf States in a continuous flight of 600 miles! And what about the

juvenile making its first trip alone? Do birds use
moon, stars, and landmarks for directional aids? We   *Navigation in migration*
human beings must use an array of sophisticated in-
struments to enable us to navigate. It has to be assumed that birds accomplish within themselves the
same protracted calculations.

There are five North American migration routes.
The Atlantic Oceanic Route runs from northeastern
Canada, Labrador, and Nova Scotia down the Atlantic to the coast of Brazil. Water and shore birds and
the golden plover fly this route, but because of the
nonstop distances over water no land birds use it.

The Atlantic Coast Route goes from northeastern
Canada to the Great Lakes, to Pennsylvania and down
by the Cheasapeake—where many birds winter—and
on to Florida, across to Cuba and the West Indies.

The Central Flyway of the Great Plains and Rocky
Mountain flyways starts in Alaska but follows the
Great Plains from Montana to New Mexico; the
Pacific Flyway also begins in Alaska and runs along
the coast and mountain valleys to the south.

What of the hardy stay-at-homes? How do they fare
in the bitter weather? Among the permanent residents   *Over-wintering birds*
and winter visitors an increasing number of individu-
als survive because they are being fed. This is an
artificial situation, but man's disturbance of the environment has created loss of food in the winter for
some species, and his feeding does help to compensate. This is true of chickadees and nuthatches. The
cardinal, who is now seen far north of his former
range, can survive only by being fed. Evening grosbeaks are winter visitors from the north who go where
the food is: where it is, so are they.

Two kinds of food are naturally available in
winter—seeds and insects. Chickadees, nuthatches,
kinglets, woodpeckers, titmice, and creepers are on

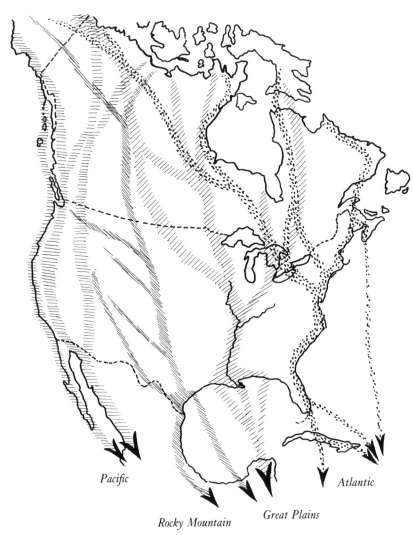

Pacific

Rocky Mountain

Great Plains

Atlantic

The principal North American migration routes

the lookout for insects that are secreted in winter buds, under bark, or on the needles of conifers.

Other foods are seeds from weeds and trees, and berries. A good share of the winter birds—the grosbeaks, mockingbirds, finches, chickadees, sparrows, and nuthatches—use these seeds and berries as their main diet.

The cold of winter is not so much a threat as is starvation: fly south or starve is the choice for a good share of birds. With protection from wind and enough to eat, birds for the most part can survive in extremely cold weather. Nuthatches, finches, juncos, chickadees will press feather to feather to wait out the long cold nights. As they spend most of the winter at the roosting place, about sixteen out of the day's twenty-four hours, they are careful to choose a sheltered spot, usually an evergreen with a thick trunk, and huddle together on the side away from the north and east winds. Tree tops are avoided because they are too exposed. As night approaches, the birds try not to get wet, for, once darkness falls, they will have no chance to dry out their feathers by flying. They lose so much body heat during the night that being wet in addition will cause many to die.

For most of us winter appears to be the best season of the year to observe birds. With a feeder close to a window and sunflower seed and cracked corn and suet available—maybe even some precious thistle seed—birds of many species soon appear. With a bird guide at hand we can soon get to know well our winter neighbors.

Pine siskin

How to Enjoy the Birds
You've Invited

The birds have accepted your invitation. Summer visitors consider your trees and bushes, and your nesting boxes as suited exactly to their requirements for family living. There is plenty of food and water available, concealment from enemies, just the right sites for their nests.

The winter birds, those who stay around all year and the others who migrate from territories farther north, find cover from bad weather and suitable food thoughtfully provided.

They are obviously enjoying your home, and you are amply rewarded by the joy of having about you some of the most fascinating creatures in the universe.

In order more fully to enjoy your visitors, you have already bought binoculars or are considering doing so. How wonderful to see the color of the legs and bill, the faint eye-stripes, as though the bird were in your hand! All those many details that can be the key to identifying difficult birds are right before your eyes.

If you're like us, you probably have no idea of what to look for in a pair of glasses. The numbers printed on them meant nothing. We didn't know even the correct way to focus them. What was the difference between a pair of binoculars and a telescope except their shape?

Binoculars have inside each barrel two sets of prisms that channel the light rays back, then redirect them forward again. In this method of using prisms the compact glasses can be shortened, and are thus handier than a telescope of the same power, and at the same time ensure the gathering of more light.

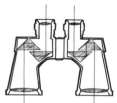

Unfortunately, the expert arrangement of the carefully ground lenses and frosted glass is a tricky business. And expensive. The more you pay for binoculars, the longer they'll last, for in relatively expensive glasses the lenses are positioned more securely. We simply could not afford the best, but so far we've been careful and haven't dropped them too hard, so they have served us well.

Using Binoculars in a Hurry

We had always focused in such a haphazard manner that no wonder we couldn't find the birds. And the trick of focusing is really so simple. The first thing is to get the glasses adjusted to the distance between your eyes. It's different in everybody: that's why the two barrels are hinged. So look at something through them with both eyes open and move them until the images of the object are merged into one. This is your own particular setting, so look at the gradations on the hinge and remember them. When you grab a pair from someone who's already spotted a wheatear, immediately move the barrels to your setting before putting the glasses to your eyes. That saves time.

Here's the best trick of all. As we know, one person's eyes differ from another's. How often we twisted those eyepieces in a vain attempt to see a bird who simply got tired of sitting around! Only one eyepiece is adjustable and has numbers on it. Turn it so that the Zero is over the guide mark. Now, keeping both eyes open, focus on an object about 500 feet off that's got lots of little details, like leaves and twigs. Block off that adjustable eyepiece and turn the center-post adjustment until the object is in clear detail. Now cover the other side and focus with the adjustable eyepiece until that, too, is clear. Remember the setting of that eye, and when you have to use the binoculars, turn it first to that setting—and then all you'll have to do is adjust the center wheel.

Eyeglass-users can find special eyecups to use with their binoculars.

Here are some tips on how to hold them up to your face. We found we were doing that the hard way, too. Fit the eyepiece against and just under the eyebrow bone, your thumbs braced under and against your cheekbones. You'll be surprised how this position can be held without tiring. Eyeglass-wearers brace their thumbs generally in the same way, but with their outstretched index fingers pressed against the forehead. Those who own pocket-size field glasses simply brace their curved index fingers against the forehead. No shaky arms and hands, everything in focus on that bird in the tree!

Magnification and field   Those mysterious numbers (7 × 35), (8 × 40), (10 × 50) have a purpose. The "7" on a 7 × 35 pair means that the cedar waxwing you're looking at is seven times as big as when you first saw him with your naked eye. In other words, he is seven times nearer you. The "35" tells the diameter of the lens in millimeters—which has to do with the width of view, the "field of view," at 1,000 yards. At such a distance with a 7- or 8-power pair, you can usually take in what's happening in a view or scene 420 feet wide. That's about all most people can deal with. With a more powerful glass the view narrows and it's more difficult to find a bird. Also, the more powerful glasses are heavier and harder to hold. The 7 × 35 is the most popular with bird watchers for that reason. If you're going in for watching ducks and water birds then a heavier, more powerful glass is what you may want. Beyond that is the world of spotting scopes, which are really more specialized than anything needed to see the birds who have come to your home.

If you're going for nature photography and have found that the weight of binoculars added to that of a camera is a nuisance, consider the fine lightweight glasses now available—they weigh as little as seven ounces. And they're compact enough to go in your pocket instead of dangling around your neck.

Taking Bird Photographs

A young friend brought to our place one weekend a huge camera of the sort beloved by Civil War photographers or used by "studio artists." It was complete with elegant mahogany tripod and black velvet cloth, and the prints from its glass negatives were superb. We spent a day carefully carrying it about, one person bearing the case, another the tripod. We treasure the beautiful black-and-white print of a woodpecker's hole, but we held our breath every time we moved the treasured antique. It was not particularly light and most definitely was clumsy. No wonder bird-lovers had to wait for the development of the 35-millimeter camera.

Even with the sophisticated instruments of today, taking good pictures of birds is no easy matter. There's that invisible barrier, the space barrier, between you. They will not let you pass it. And it's impossible to follow the birds about, hoping that they'll freeze long enough for you to trip the shutter. Impossible, that is, unless you have intricate equipment and years of experience behind you.

But if you, an amateur, are determined to take bird pictures, there are ways to go about it.

First you have to lure the birds to your own territory so you can photograph them on your terms. You do this by setting up a feeder four feet from a window with a southerly exposure. If at all possible there should be a mass of trees or some natural background four feet beyond the feeder, to let the bird be in focus against a vague mass that is indistinguishable. To make the scene as real as possible, attach branches to the feeder so that, when the bird lands on them, he will be sideways or at a 45-degree angle, the best angle at which to catch birds.

The feeder need not be large, just a two-foot shelf. Scatter feed on the ground until the ground-feeders get used to the shelf and will perch on top. It should be placed where it gets sun, but have cover at least on one side. Water may be put out too.

Camera equipment   Now for the equipment. An absolute minimum must be a single-lens 35 mm camera with interchangeable lenses, and a 2× tele extender which makes the camera into a 135 mm with a focal length of 270 mm. For color photos, use high-speed Ektachrome film, ASA 160 or 164. Don't try to hand-hold the camera: use a tripod that's had its rubber pads, if any, re-

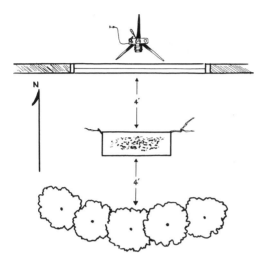

Winter bird photo set-up

moved; be sure the legs are on bare floor. Use a cable release to the shutter to prevent any vibration from your finger.

Poke the camera through an open window that can be blocked off if necessary.

The best time for photographing birds is in the early morning, or fairly late in the afternoon: sidelighting is dramatic and gives good modeling to the feathers. Focus on the bird's eye, the sharpest light on a bird. In photographer's language, this is the "catch light."

It does seem to be a complicated procedure, but if you're determined to try to get pictures yourself, this is the way to start.

The Fun of Records

Part of the pleasure of inviting birds is reviewing the year-by-year counts of winter birds. Record such facts as where they roosted at night, when they came to feed and in what sequence, when they drank, and when they sat in the sun to enjoy its warmth. You'll be surprised by how much you've learned by observing and noting carefully these rather obvious happenings.

Bird watching   The arrival of the migrating birds in the spring is one of the most exciting events in the year and never seems to lose its magic. Our very first blackbird's *ok-a-lee* stops us short in the midst of our daily rush just as it did years ago. In the fall the quiet, almost unnoticed stealing away one by one of the summer birds leaves us pensive and nostalgic, and in a fitting mood for autumn and its grey days.

Keeping records of the spring migration is easy: the birds are full of exuberance and announce their arrival with gusto. But during the fall flitting, you can only note their absence. In the summer, try to notice where they nest and how many broods they have.

The best time for seeing birds is at "first light," and in midsummer this means rising early. You'll be amply repaid for the effort. Birds have sharp eyes, much sharper than ours, for their lives depend on this vision, so it behooves you to walk or stand as quietly as possible. Rob Jarvis, when he took us walking, made us keep our hands clasped behind us, a worthwhile precaution when you stop to realize how we tend to gesticulate and move our hands. Even lifting binoculars is likely to send the bird flitting off. Birds have color sense—their bright courting colors tell us that—so wear subdued clothing that doesn't flap about. Speak quietly, and keep the young children and dogs at home. This is where the trick comes in of saying quietly its identification points. The best thing of all is to sit or prop yourself up in one place and just wait—almost an impossible feat for our frantic generation! But look and listen and you'll realize that all about you are creatures living their lives, unnoticed by bustling, hurried human beings.

Calling to Birds

Naturalists have long known that they could "call" a bird or birds by squeaking against the back of the hand, making a sort of kissing noise. This often arouses the curiosity of a bird so that he will answer, giving you a chance to identify him; or he will hop over to see what this odd new bird is. Now there's a whistle, called a squeaker, that makes a variety of calls. But be warned that a squeaker sometimes brings more than just birds to investigate—perhaps a curious and hungry snake!

Most sophisticated of all is the tape machine with recorded bird calls that is small enough to be used in the field. Miss Riley came one spring day to show us the new device that had been given to her by her class as a wedding present. "Let's try it on Father Catbird," suggested Katie.

Father was busily helping to put together a new nest in the old lilac and didn't pay much attention to us, whose lilac it was. Miss Riley found the catbird call and song and turned it on while we stood on the lawn. It was almost like playing a dirty trick on an old friend. Mr. Catbird dropped his mouthful of carefully selected twigs and rushed to the nearest apple tree, where he proceeded to give us and the tape a piece of his mind. "What do you mean, you intruder, coming onto my property like this! I've been here for years. This is my place and I intend that only I and my family will live here. Now *get OFF!*" He seemed to be glaring at us until Miss Riley let the tape run into the

Tape recorders

call of another bird whose simulated presence appeared not to concern the catbird at all. Satisfied that he had driven off the intruder, he went back to gathering up nest twigs.

Tape recorders are a fine way of getting birds to come close, but it is important to be responsible about their use. Don't keep an angry male on a branch above you hopping with fury; prolonged anger isn't any better for him than for you.

Join a nature club and participate in the group's activities. You'll find not only knowledge, but friendship. Many of these clubs have "bird lines," a telephone number to call to let them know about any unusual bird you've seen. Usually, in return, a taped message will tell you what species are being sighted by others.

Bird censuses   Participation in the National Christmas Bird Count is a fine way of helping to monitor the advancement of some species into new areas, and how they are affecting the native populations. House sparrows, house finches, mockingbirds, cardinals, starlings, cattle egrets, all have moved into territories that are new to them.

The bird censuses and the hawk watches warn us that the declining populations of certain birds are an indication that long-lived pesticides and herbicides are having a baneful effect on the environment that we all share. Keeping a watch on the numbers of geese, duck, and game birds tells us how our wild and wet lands are faring.

We've come a long way from the days when in order to identify birds the naturalist had to shoot them. Now we collect by sight or camera.

Here are a few tricks to make sighting easier. When a flock of geese stream overhead, or when you want to count a raft of eiders, don't despair. You can learn to make a pretty fair reckoning of numbers by gently throwing a small handful of beans on a flat surface, and making an estimate of their number. Do this repeatedly, observing the scatter pattern, and soon you'll be able to make an accurate guess at the numbers in a flock.

Here's how you make easier that difficult task of indicating to another person just where a certain bird is. Don't point—it scares the birds. Instead, pick out a natural object near the bird and use it as an imaginary clock face. "See that dead tree, that's the center of the clock. The bird is at nine o'clock."

Judging distance is something I used to have trouble with. Guests have spent hours roaming back roads following the directions I gave. Now I'm pretty accurate. This is the way you do it. Choose a distance that you see every day, the tennis court next door or your own front walk. Pace it off, one yard to a long step, and look at it frequently, saying to yourself, "That walk is ten yards long." When that distance is established in your mind, you can say that a bird is three "walks," or thirty yards, away.

The very best advice of all is to take time to enjoy the rich world around you. It's all about and it's free for the seeing and looking and loving.

A Plurality of Birds

These terms have come down to us over the centuries to describe birds in groups, and some are still in use today:

A badelyng of duck
A bazaar of murres (guillemots)
A bevy of quail
A brood of chickens
A cast of hawks
A charm of finches
A chattering of choughs
A company of widgeon
A congregation of plover
A covert of coots
A covey of partridge
A desert of lapwings
An exaltation of larks
A fall of woodcock
A flight of doves or swallows
A gaggle of geese
A herd of cranes, curlews, or swans
A host of sparrows
A murder of crows
A murmuration of starlings
A muster of peacocks
A nye of pheasant
A plump of wildfowl
A siege of bitterns or herons
A skein of geese (flying)
A sord of mallard
A spring of teal
A trip of dotterel (plover)
A watch of nightingales
A wisp (or walk) of snipe

APPENDIX B

A List of Helpful Books

Bull, John, and John Farrand, Jr. *Audubon Society Field Guide to North American Birds*, Vol. I, *Eastern Region*. New York: Alfred Knopf, 1977.

Uvardy, M. D. *Audubon Society Field Guide to North American Birds*, Vol. II, *Western Region*. New York: Alfred Knopf, 1977.

(Both volumes are illustrated with photographs. Critics complain that photos portray an individual, whereas a painting generalizes differences created by age and locality, thus making identification of the species easier for a beginner. The books also group birds by look-alikes, disregarding family groups. They are great fun to read, though.)

Forbush, Edward. *Birds of Massachusetts and Other New England States*. 3 vols. Boston: 1929.

(This monumental work, commissioned by the Commonwealth of Massachusetts, is now, alas, out of print. Illustrated beautifully by Louis Fuertes, with its detailed descriptions and wonderful stories it is well worth while getting from a library.)

Harrison, Hal. *Field Guide to Birds' Nest East of the Mississippi River*. Boston: Houghton Mifflin, 1975.

(Nest identification is almost as much fun as identifying the maker.)

Hickey, Joseph H. *Guide to Bird Watching*. New York: Dover Press, 1975

(A classic on where to go and how to watch birds.)

Hickman, Mae, and Maxine Guy. *Care of the Wild Feathered and Furred, a Guide to Wildlife Handling and Care*. Santa Cruz: Unity Press, 1973.

(Careful and sensible step-by-step explanation of how to deal with emergencies.)

Martin, Alfred G. *Hand-Taming Wild Birds at the Feeder.* Freeport, Maine: Bond Wheelwright Company, 1963.
(This book has useful information although many feel that coaxing birds to come to you is stepping through the natural barrier that separates human beings and wild things.)

Peterson, Roger Troy. *Field Guide to Eastern Land and Water Birds*, 2nd ed. Boston: Houghton Mifflin, 1947. Paper edition, 1968.
(It was in this guide that Peterson developed his famous identification points, which are available in no other bird guides. At this writing the projected revised edition will place illustration and text on facing pages, thus eliminating the need to flip back and forth through book.)
———. *Field Guide to Birds of Texas and Adjacent States.* Boston: Houghton Mifflin, 1963.
———. *The Birds.* New York: Time Incorporated, 1963.
(Invaluable reading if you want to know how a bird flies, eats and nests: everything from fossils to feathers.)
———. *Field Guide to Western Birds.* Boston: Houghton Mifflin, 1972.
———. *Gardening with Wildlife.* Washington, D.C.: World Wildlife Foundation, 1974.
(How to plan and plant your property to attract birds and other creatures.)

Pough, Richard H. *Audubon Land Bird Guide, Small Land Birds of Eastern and Central North America from Southern Texas to Central Greenland*, rev. ed. Garden City: Doubleday, 1951.

————. *Audubon Water Bird Guide, Water, Game and Large Land Birds.* Garden City: Doubleday, 1951.

Robbins, Chandler S., et al. *Birds of North America, A Guide to Field Identification.* New York: Golden Press, 1966.

(The great advantage to this guide is that it covers the whole continent in one volume and has text and illustration on facing pages.)

Terres, John. *Song Birds in Your Garden*, rev. ed. New York: T. Y. Crowell, 1968.

(Amusing, well written, lots of ideas.)

Wetmore, Alexander, et al. *Song and Garden Birds of North America.* Washington, D.C.: National Geographic Society, 1975.

(Plentifully illustrated, this lavish volume gives full and detailed descriptions of songbirds. A very good reference book.)

Government Publications

The following may be obtained from the Superintendent of Documents, U.S. Government Printing Office, Washington, D.C. 20402. To save time, check the current lists at your County Extension Service office to be certain of the correct price.

Invite Birds to Your Home:
  Conservation Plantings for the Midwest, PA 982.
  Conservation Plantings for the Northwest, PA 1094.
  Conservation Plantings for the Southeast, PA 1093.
  Conservation Plantings for the Northeast, PA 940

Selecting and Growing Shade Trees, G 205.
Shrubs, Vines and Trees . . . for Summer Color, G 181.
Transplanting Ornamental Trees and Shrubs, G 192.
More Wildlife through Soil and Water, AB 175.

RECORDINGS

A set of two records or two cassettes may be bought to go with Peterson's *Guide to Eastern Land and Water Birds*.

Three records or cassettes may be bought with Peterson's *Field Guide to Western Birds*.

The National Geographic Society offers for sale an album of six records to go with *Song and Garden Birds of North America*.

APPENDIX C

Glossary

Accipiter   Any hawk that has short round wings and a long tail and that feeds chiefly on small mammals and birds.

Addle   To cause to lose ability to develop; to make muddled or become spoiled or rotten, as eggs.

Altricial   Helpless at hatching, and requiring parental care for a period of time; early flying.

Archaeopteryx   A fossil bird from the late Jurassic Period, having teeth and a long, feathered vertebrate tail; the oldest known avian type.

Brood patch (or *incubation patch*)   Featherless area with a great many blood vessels, developed on the abdomen of certain birds; it comes in direct contact with eggs during incubation and provides additional warmth.

Buteo   Any large hawk with broad wings and broad, rounded tail, which habitually soars, in wide circles, high in the air.

Clutch   A nestful of eggs that will be incubated when the female finishes laying. The number varies from species to species.

Coniferous   Cone-bearing; mostly evergreen trees.

Deciduous   Shedding the leaves annually (trees, shrubs, etc.).

Diurnal   Active by day, as certain birds and insects; *see also* Nocturnal.

Egg tooth   A calcareous prominence at the tip of the beak or upper jaw of an embryonic bird or reptile, used to break through the shell at hatching.

Family   The usual major subdivision of an order or suborder in the classification of plants and animals, usually consisting of several genera; *see* Genus.

Fledgling   Young bird just fledged, i.e., having the plumage necessary for flight.

Genus (pl. *genera*)   The usual major subdivision of a family or subfamily in the classification of plants and animals, generally consisting of more than one species.

Juvenile   Term used to describe any immature plumage or immature bird.

Miocene   Noting or pertaining to an epoch either of the Tertiary or Neocene period, occurring from 10 million to 25 million years ago and characterized by the presence of vast grassy areas which fostered the development of birds.

Molt   To shed and replace plumage.

Nocturnal   Active by night, usually as opposed to active by day.

Order   Classification group composed of related families.

Passerine   Belonging or pertaining to the order Passeriformes (comprising more than half of all birds), typically having the feet adapted for perching.

Phylum (pl. *phyla*)   The major subdivision of the animal kingdom consisting of one or more related classes.

Precocial   Active, down-covered, and able to move about freely when hatched; late flying.

Raptor   Preying upon other animals; predatory. Adapted for seizing prey, as with the bill or claws of a bird.

Species   A group of similar individuals that interbreeds within itself, but not with individuals of other such groups.

Taxonomy   The science or technique of classification.

Index

Accipiter, *ill. 78*
American Ornithological
    Union (AOU), 110

Bath(s), 69–72
  see also Watering
Binoculars, 135–137, *ill. 135*
Bird(s)
  berry-eaters, 45–46
  biological overview,
    73–76, 86–88, 112–114
  flesh-eaters, *ill. 44*
  information sources,
    46–47, 48–49
  insect eaters, 51, *ill. 43*
  nursing, 37
  non-nursing, 37
  orders of birds, 112–114
  perchers, 29
  seed-eaters, 44–45,
    55–56, *ills. 43, 44*
  sense of smell, 97
  victims of progress, 86–94
Bird calls, 19–20
  see also specific species
Bird "houses," *see* Nesting boxes
Blackbird(s)
  call, 2–3
  camouflage, 10
  diet, 10
  nest, 9
  nesting, 10
  red-winged, *ill. 1*
Bluebird(s)
  nesting box specifications, 122
  nesting needs, 91–92
  victims of progress, 91
Bluejay(s), feeding habits, 81–82
Brooding
  "brood patch," 33
  "determinate layers," 29
  incubation timetable, 29

  laying timetable, 30
  mechanics of, 32, 34
  temperature for, 34
  see also Eggs, Hatching
Buteo, *ill. 78*

Calling birds, 141–142
Camouflage, *see* specific species
Cardinal(s)
  favorite annuals, 61–62
  wintering over, 132
Catbird(s)
  brooding, 32
  early development, 36–41
  feeding by parents, 36–37
  gray, *ill. 28*
  nest(s), 30–31
  nesting, 32
Cat-proofing, 82, *ill. 82*
Cedar waxwing, *ill. 42*
Chickadee(s)
  black-capped, *ill. 12*
  favorite annuals, 62
  nesting box specifications, 122
Club(s), 142
Counts, (bird)
  how to participate, 142
  purpose, 142
  sighting tricks, 142–143
Cowbird(s), nesting, 26–27
Crows, feeding habits, 81–82

"Doctoring"
  a broken leg, 104, *ills. 99, 106*
  a fallen nestling, 96–103
  feeding the invalid, 102
  make-do nest, 98–99
  rescuing the older bird, 103
  signing out the patient, 102
  what about wings, 107
  when doctoring fails, 107
Dove, white-winged, call, 19